Understanding and Mastering
The Bluebook®

Understanding and Mastering
The Bluebook®

A Guide for Students and Practitioners

FOURTH EDITION

Linda J. Barris

CAROLINA ACADEMIC PRESS
Durham, North Carolina

Library of Congress Cataloging-in-Publication Data

Names: Barris, Linda J., author.
Title: Understanding and mastering the bluebook : a guide for students and practitioners /
    by Linda J. Barris.
Description: Fourth edition. | Durham, North Carolina : Carolina Academic Press, LLC,
    [2020] | Includes index.
Identifiers: LCCN 2020005221 | ISBN 9781531019150 (spiral bound) |
    ISBN 9781531019167 (ebook)
Subjects: LCSH: Citation of legal authorities—United States. | Annotations and
    citations (Law)—United States.
Classification: LCC KF245 .B37 2020 | DDC 808.02/7—dc23
LC record available at https://lccn.loc.gov/2020005221

ISBN 978-1-5310-2403-1 (perfectbound paperback)

Carolina Academic Press
700 Kent Street
Durham, NC 27701
(919) 489-7486
www.cap-press.com

This book is published as a guide to the rules of legal citation set forth in *The Bluebook: A Uniform System of Citation,* Twenty-First Edition, copyright 2020 by The Columbia Law Review Association, The Harvard Law Review, the University of Pennsylvania Law Review, and The Yale Law Journal. This book is neither published by nor affiliated with the publishers of *The Bluebook. The Bluebook* is published by The Harvard Law Review Association, Gannett House, 1511 Massachusetts Avenue, Cambridge, MA 02138.

Printed in 2021

Contents

Keeping Up to Date   **xi**

Acknowledgments   **xiii**

1 Getting Started   **3**
   A. Introduction to Legal Citation and *The Bluebook*   4
      1. The Purpose of Legal Citation   4
      2. *Bluebook* Organization   5
   B. Practitioners' Style and Local Rules   6
      1. Typeface Conventions: Practitioners' Style   6
      2. Introduction to Local Rules   9
   C. When to Cite   10
   D. Citation Sentences, Clauses, and Embedded Citations   12
      1. Citation Sentences   14
      2. Citation Clauses   14
      3. Embedded Citations   15
   E. Pinpoint Citations   17
      1. Pages   18
      2. Sections and Subsections   19
      3. Paragraphs   21
      4. Lines   21
      5. Footnotes   22
      6. Endnotes   23
      7. Supplements   24
   F. Spacing Rules for Citation Abbreviations   24
   G. Introduction to Short Form Citations   26
      1. *Id.*   26
      2. *Supra*   27
      3. Alternate Short Forms   28

2 Cases   **29**
   A. Basic Case Citation Rules   30
      1. Case Name   30
      2. Source Information   33
         (a) Volume   35

(b) Reporter Name   35
(c) Beginning Page Number   35
(d) Pinpoint Page Number (aka Pincite)   35
3. Court   36
4. Year   39
B. Special Rules for Case Names   40
1. Businesses and Organizations   40
2. Governmental Parties (Geographical Terms)   42
(a) Federal Government   43
(b) State Governments   44
(c) A County, City, or Town Is a Party   46
3. Alternate Names   47
4. Procedural and Descriptive Phrases   47
5. Unions   51
6. Commissioner of Internal Revenue   52
C. Short Form Case Citations   52
1. Id.   52
2. Alternate Short Form   53
D. Parallel Citations   58
E. Public Domain Citations   59
F. Parenthetical Information   62
1. Dissents and Concurrences   62
2. Quoting or Citing Parentheticals   63
3. Weight of Authority   64
G. Subsequent History   65
H. Ordering Multiple Additions to Citations   66

3 Statutes   **67**
A. Federal and State Statutes   68
1. Form   68
2. Basic Statutory Citations   70
3. Code Name   70
4. Titles, Chapters, and Section Numbers   71
5. Publisher   74
6. Year of Code   75
B. Additional Information in Statutory Citations   76
1. Supplements   76
2. Subject Matter Codes   77
3. Named Statutes   77

C. Short Forms: Statutes   77
  1. Id.   78
  2. Alternate Short Form   79

4 Constitutions   **81**
A. Basic Citation Forms   81
B. Short Form: Constitutions   82

5 Regulations   **85**
A. Federal Administrative Regulations   85
B. State Administrative Regulations   87
C. Internal Revenue Code   88
D. Treasury Regulations   90

6 Procedural and Court Rules   **93**
A. Rules of Procedure and Evidence   93
  1. Federal Rules of Procedure and Evidence   93
  2. State Rules of Procedure and Evidence   94
B. Rules of Court   95
  1. Federal Rules of Court   95
  2. State Rules of Court   96
C. Short Forms: Rules   97

7 Secondary Sources   **99**
A. Treatises and Books   99
  1. Author's Full Name   100
  2. Book Title   101
  3. Pinpoint Page, Section, or Volume   101
  4. Publication Information   101
  5. Year   102
  6. Short Forms: Treatises and Books   102
B. Periodicals (Law Reviews and Journals)   103
  1. Author's Full Name   104
  2. Article Title   104
  3. Volume   105
  4. Periodical Name   105
  5. Beginning Page   106
  6. Pinpoint Page(s)   106
  7. Year   106
  Short Forms: Periodicals   106

C. Restatements 108
 Short Forms: Restatements 109
D. Legal Dictionaries 110
 Short Forms: Dictionaries 111
E. American Law Reports (A.L.R.) Annotations 112
 Short Forms: A.L.R. Annotations 113
F. Legal Encyclopedias 114
 Short Forms: Encyclopedias 114

8 Litigation Documents and Record Citations **117**
A. Litigation Documents and Appellate Record 117
 1. Document Title 118
 2. Pinpoint Citations 119
B. Short Forms: Litigation and Record Citations 120
C. Enclosing Citations in Parentheses 121

9 Strings, Signals, and Explanatory Parentheticals **123**
A. String Citations 123
 1. String Basics 123
 2. Short Forms in String Citations 125
B. Signals 126
 1. Signal Basics 127
 2. Using Multiple Signals in a Single String 129
 3. Using Short Forms with Signals 131
C. Explanatory Parentheticals 131

10 Quotations **135**
A. Form of Quotations 135
 1. Block Quotations 136
 2. Short Quotations 136
B. Alterations 137
C. Omissions 139

11 Capitalization **143**
A. Capitalization Basics 143
B. Court Documents and Proceedings 145
 1. Courts 145
 2. Parties to a Legal Action 146
 3. Titles of Court Documents 147
 4. Court Proceedings 147
 5. Judges 147

12 Numbers, Numerals, Ordinals, and Symbols   149
   A. Numbers and Numerals   149
   B. Ordinals   151
   C. Symbols   151

13 Electronic Sources   153
   A. Cases   155
      1. Commercial Databases: Published Decisions   156
      2. Commercial Databases: Unpublished Decisions   157
      3. Authenticated or Official Decisions   160
   B. Statutes   160
      1. Commercial Databases   160
      2. Authenticated or Official Versions   161
      3. Short Forms   161
      4. Practitioners' Alternate Form (Optional)   162
   C. Constitutions   163
   D. Regulations   164
   E. Procedural and Court Rules   165
   F. Secondary Sources   166
      1. Treatises and Books   166
      2. Periodicals   167
      3. Restatements   168
      4. Dictionaries   168
      5. A.L.R. Annotations   169
      6. Encyclopedias   170

Appendix: Citing Cases from Commercial Databases   171

Index of *Bluebook* Rules   175

Subject Index   177

Keeping Up to Date

From time to time, the editors of *The Bluebook* announce minor rule changes, correct errors in examples, or revise entries in the White Pages tables. When these changes affect practitioners' citations, an online update to *Understanding and Mastering* The Bluebook is posted.

To check for updates, visit: caplaw.com/umb.

Acknowledgments

A special thanks to the many legal writing instructors, librarians, colleagues, and friends who have offered insight and feedback over the years.

Understanding and Mastering
The Bluebook

1 Getting Started

If you have cracked open *The Bluebook*, you already know that it presents a bewildering assortment of rules, rules, and more rules for legal citation. If you are new to legal citation, or a little rusty at it, the task of deciphering and applying those rules can seem overwhelming. This book is designed to help you learn basic *Bluebook* citation form and how to use *The Bluebook* manual. By breaking citations down into individual steps and pulling together rules scattered throughout *The Bluebook*, the task of preparing citations in correct *Bluebook* form is much easier to understand—and master.

Chapter 1 of this guide reviews the concepts and purposes of legal citation, and introduces a few citation rules and principles applying to most citations, no matter what type of authority is cited. This introductory chapter includes the following:

A. Introduction to legal citation and the *Bluebook*, beginning on page 4;

B. Introduction to Practitioner's Style, and local rules, beginning on page 6;

C. When to cite, beginning on page 10;

D. Where to place the citation, including citation sentences, clauses, and embedded citations, beginning on page 12;

E. Pinpoint cites to specific pages, sections, paragraphs, lines, supplements, or footnotes, beginning on page 17;

F. Spacing in citation abbreviations, beginning on page 24; and

G. Introduction to short form citations, beginning on page 26.

About This Guide

This guidebook is designed to help you learn how to use *The Bluebook*, but it is not—and is not meant to be—a substitute for *The Bluebook* itself. The citation forms described in this guide are basic forms only. As you will learn, there are many exceptions to the basic rules, and many less-common rules and sources that this guide is not designed to cover. Cross references in this guide point to the *Bluebook* rules pertaining to the topic under discussion. Be sure to use those cross references because there is simply no substitute for digging into *The Bluebook* and learning to decipher its rules.

This guide follows the 21st edition of *The Bluebook*. Make sure your copy of *The Bluebook* is the 21st edition.

Box continues on the next page.

About This Guide, *continued*

Throughout this guide certain conventions have been employed:

● Indicates a Basic Rule.

✘ Indicates an Exception to the Basic Rule.

☞ Points to a tip, example, or helpful information about a particular rule.

♦ Indicates that *The Bluebook* allows alternatives, or that customary practice may deviate from *Bluebook* rules. Always follow your instructor's or supervisor's preferred style or practice.

☞ *The Bluebook* itself has a citation form: <u>The Bluebook: A Uniform System of Citation</u> R. 15.8(c)(v), at 154 (Columbia Law Review Ass'n et al. eds., 21st ed. 2020). Throughout this guide you will see references to *Bluebook* rules using a short form citation method. Look for: *Bluebook* R. 15.8 or simply Rule 15.8.

☞ Many of the examples in this guide use **boldface type** to help illustrate rules. **DO NOT USE BOLDFACE IN ANY PART OF YOUR CITATIONS.**

☞ Some examples include gray numbers [2], gray dots [•], or vertical lines [|]. These are for illustration purposes only—do not include in your citation.

A. Introduction to Legal Citation and *The Bluebook*

Before learning how to create legal citations, it is important to understand the purpose of legal citation, as it may differ from the purpose of citations you have created in the past.

1. The Purpose of Legal Citation

The purpose of legal citation is threefold: (1) to indicate that you are relying upon authority; (2) to identify the specific authority relied upon and its weight or persuasiveness; and (3) to provide an easy way to locate a copy of the authority.

As noted, the first purpose of citation is to let your reader know that the statement you have just made is based upon authority. If you make an assertion about the law and do not immediately follow with a citation, your reader will assume that whatever you just wrote is your personal opinion. Good legal analysis is based on law, not personal opinion. Using citations tells the reader that the statement is backed by authority.

The second function of legal citation is to identify the authority relied upon and indicate how it fits in with other rules of authority in the United States. Not all authorities are created equal. Some authorities such as a Constitution or United States Supreme Court case, are usually more "important" or "persuasive" than cases from lower courts or state authorities. Your citation will tell the reader exactly where the authority fits into the pecking order of all authorities.

The third purpose of citation is to provide all the information needed to quickly locate the cited authority. There are millions of different authorities a legal writer can cite including cases, statutes, regulations, treatises, and legal articles, to name just a few. Law libraries are stuffed with volume after volume of legal authorities. Online resources offer even more. Legal citations point readers straight to the original source enabling them to go directly to the specific book on the library shelf—or click a few computer keys— and open to the exact spot in the authority where you obtained your information.

2. Bluebook Organization

To understand how *The Bluebook* is organized, it helps to know a little of its history. The citation manual was first published in 1926 to provide rules for academic writers writing articles published in law reviews, journals, or books on specialized legal topics. As *The Bluebook*'s subtitle indicates, it provided a "uniform system of citation" so that all academic writers used the same formats for their citations.

Some years after the initial publication of *The Bluebook*, practicing attorneys began using The Bluebook as a guide for uniform citations in documents they submitted to courts, adapting some of the rules to fit their needs. *The Bluebook*'s publisher eventually responded by developing the Bluepages in the front of the manual to specifically address practitioners' needs.

Take a few minutes to familiarize yourself with the type of information in the 21st edition of *The Bluebook* and how that information is organized. The two charts below show: (1) the general organization of *The Bluebook* rules, and (2) the tools available to help you find the specific rules governing your citation.

The Rules

Bluepages • Also known as **Practitioners' Notes.** • Bluepages rules are identified by the "B" prefix. ***Example:*** **B5.1.**	This section translates the rules found in the Whitepages (Academic Style) into Practitioners' Style. It also provides rules unique to Practitioners' Style such as citing court documents. Tables in the back of the Bluepages list common abbreviations and sources for local rules affecting practitioners' citations.
Rules Pages • Also known as the **Whitepages.** • Whitepages rules have no prefix. ***Example:*** 5.1.	This section contains rules for Academic Style. If the Bluepages do not provide a rule for practitioners, use the Whitepages rule.
Tables Pages • Table rules are identified by the "T" prefix. ***Example:*** T6.	This section provides information about and abbreviations for numerous authorities. A quick list of the tables is located on the back cover.

The Tools to Find the Rules

Table of Contents *In the front*	To find general rules about citing specific authorities, start here. ***Example:*** *"How do I cite a case?"*
Index *In the back*	For a specific rule, start here. ***Example:*** *"How do I cite a footnote in a case?"*
Quick Reference: Law Review Footnotes *Inside front cover*	Use this reference only if you are writing a law review article. ☞ Practitioners do not use this reference.
Quick Reference: Court Documents and Legal Memoranda *Inside back cover*	Use this reference to quickly find the general form for citations using Practitioners' Style, and to cross-reference Whitepages rules.
Quick Index *Outside back cover*	The quickest way to find the general rules. Also contains a helpful list of the Tables.

B. Practitioners' Style and Local Rules

Practicing lawyers writing legal memoranda or briefs must adapt some *Bluebook* rules from the Academic Style, found in the Whitepages, to a style suitable for use in a law office or court. These adaptations are described in the Bluepages found at the beginning of *The Bluebook*. This section discusses the following adaptations practitioners must make:

1. Conforming typefaces to Practitioners' Style, beginning on this page; and

2. Conforming citations to local rules or customs, beginning on page 9.

☞ This guide pulls together the Whitepages and Bluepages rules so that all practitioners' adaptations are discussed with the general rule. However, this guide does not cover every rule or citation situation you will encounter, so always check the Bluepages, Whitepages, and tables.

1. Typeface Conventions: Practitioners' Style   Rule B2

The Bluebook uses several typefaces for different kinds of authorities. In the Rules section of *The Bluebook* (Whitepages), you will see citations in ordinary roman type, *italics*, and LARGE AND SMALL CAPITALS.

Traditionally, all italics shown in *Bluebook* rules were converted to underlining in practitioners' citations. *The Bluebook* now permits the use of either. Some practitioners prefer underlining;

others prefer italics. Ask your instructor or supervisor which typeface he or she prefers. **Do not mix typefaces.** Once you have decided to use italics or underlining, use that style consistently throughout the document.

☞ This guide uses <u>underlining</u> in citation examples for the simple reason that it makes the examples easier to read.

Academic writers also used SMALL CAPITALS for some citation parts, including names of codes, authors of books, and others. Practitioners traditionally did not use SMALL CAPITALS because typewriters were unable to produce them. Instead, the text was converted to ordinary type. *The Bluebook* has now authorized the use of SMALL CAPITALS by practitioners, although it continues to convert the style to ordinary type in the Bluepages.

Should You Use Small Capitals?

The permissive use of SMALL CAPITALS was new to the last edition of *The Bluebook* published in 2015. As the rule change is still new, many readers of your documents are not yet accustomed to the change, or might not even be aware of it. To them, the citation may look "wrong." As with any optional *Bluebook* rule, consider your reader first. If you think the reader may believe the citation is wrongly formatted, forego the use of SMALL CAPITALS. Ask your instructor or supervisor what style is preferred.

☞ **This guide uses ordinary type, not SMALL CAPITALS, for all practitioner's citations.**

Typeface Examples

Whitepages Typefaces	Example of Whitepages Typefaces (Academic Style)	Example of Bluepages Typefaces (Practitioners' Style)
Ordinary (Roman)	This sentence is typed in ordinary (roman) type. So is this one.	Retain ordinary type in Practitioners' Style.
Italics	*This sentence is typed in italics.* *So is this one.*	♦ *Leave in italics*, or convert to ordinary type and <u>underline</u>.
LARGE AND SMALL CAPITALS	THESE SENTENCES ARE TYPED IN LARGE AND SMALL CAPITALS. NOTICE THAT THE FIRST LETTER OF EACH SENTENCE IS A SLIGHTLY LARGER CAPITAL.	♦ Convert to ordinary type (preferred). <u>Underline</u> or *italicize* as required. See chart below.

Comparison of Academic and Practitioners' Styles

Type of Authority	How a Citation Appears Following Whitepages Rules (Academic Style)	How a Citation Appears Following Bluepages Rules (Practitioners' Style)
Cases Rule 10	Metzler v. Rowell, 547 S.E.2d 311, 314 (Ga. Ct. App. 2001). ☞ Ordinary type used for case name.	Metzler v. Rowell, 547 S.E.2d 311, 314 (Ga. Ct. App. 2001). ***OR*** *Metzler v. Rowell*, 547 S.E.2d 311, 314 (Ga. Ct. App. 2001). ♦ Underline or *italicize* case name.
Statutes Rule 12	Oʜɪᴏ Rᴇᴠ. Cᴏᴅᴇ Aɴɴ. § 2911.01 (West 2018). ☞ Code title written in Sᴍᴀʟʟ Cᴀᴘɪᴛᴀʟs.	Ohio Rev. Code Ann. § 2911.01 (West 2018). ☞ Convert small capitals to ordinary type (preferred).
Books Rule 15	Eᴅᴡᴀʀᴅ E. Pᴇᴏᴘʟᴇs, Bᴀsɪᴄ Cʀɪᴍɪ-ɴᴀʟ Pʀᴏᴄᴇᴅᴜʀᴇ 29–30 (2000). ☞ Author and book title written in Sᴍᴀʟʟ Cᴀᴘɪᴛᴀʟs.	Edward E. Peoples, Basic Criminal Procedure 29–30 (2000). ***OR*** Edward E. Peoples, *Basic Criminal Procedure* 29–30 (2000). ☞ Convert small capitals to ordinary type (preferred). ♦ Underline or *italicize* title.
Periodicals Rule 16	Youngjae Lee, *The Constitutional Rights Against Excessive Punishment*, 91 Vᴀ. L. Rᴇᴠ. 677, 682 (2005). ☞ Article title written in *italics*. ☞ Periodical name written in Sᴍᴀʟʟ Cᴀᴘɪᴛᴀʟs.	Youngjae Lee, The Constitutional Rights Against Excessive Punishment, 91 Va. L. Rev. 677, 682 (2005). ***OR*** Youngjae Lee, *The Constitutional Rights Against Excessive Punishment*, 91 Va. L. Rev. 677, 682 (2005). ♦ Leave title in *italics* or convert to underlining. ☞ Convert small capitals to ordinary type (preferred).

♦ **Reminder:** *The Bluebook* permits the use of either underlining or italics. Some practitioners prefer the use of underlining, while others prefer italics. Ask your instructor or supervisor which typeface he or she prefers. Do not mix typefaces.

2. Introduction to Local Rules

The introduction to the Bluepages states that "[m]any courts have their own rules of citation differing in some respects from *The Bluebook*. Make sure you are familiar with and abide by any additional or different citation requirements of the court to which you are submitting your documents." The Bluebook: A Uniform System of Citation 3 (Columbia Law Review Ass'n et al. eds., 21st ed. 2020).

When practicing law in a specific jurisdiction, you will encounter these additional or different citation requirements, often termed "local rules" of citation. If you are a student, your instructor may ask you to conform your citations to *The Bluebook* as you learn citation, even though practitioners in your area may follow different rules. Once you learn the basics of *Bluebook* citation it is easy to make modifications to conform your citations to local rules.

For times when local rules are required, the chart below provides a quick guide to finding those rules.

How to Find Court Rules

The best source for local citation requirements is the court's own website. Here are some places to look for local rules.

1. *Bluebook* Table 1 includes entries for the main court website for each jurisdiction. The main website will usually provide links to the state's procedural and court rules, as well as links to individual courts in the jurisdiction which may have separate rules.

2. Search the Internet using the name of the court plus the phrase "court rules" as search terms.

3. Once you have found the appropriate website and located the jurisdiction's rules:

    (a) Check Bluepages Table BT2, which provides a list of citation rules for the jurisdiction. The entry will provide the rule number(s) to look up on the website.

    (b) If the rule you are looking for is not listed in Table BT2, look in the rules index on the court's website (most courts index their rules).

    (c) If you cannot find the rule listed in the rules index, look for likely spots. If the court has specific citation rules, they are usually found in the first few rules, perhaps labeled as introductory, prefatory, or miscellaneous rules. Or, use the "find" feature of your browser to search for "cite" or "citation."

☞ Both local rules and web addresses are subject to frequent change, and what is here today may be gone tomorrow. If the website has moved and there is no new link, try a different source.

C. When to Cite

- **Basic Rule:** Provide a citation for ANYTHING you take from ANY type of primary authority, secondary source, or other publication. Cite anything you take from:

  - Cases, including facts, rules, holdings, explanations, dicta, or any other information or idea taken directly from a case.

  - Statutes, constitutions, administrative rules, procedural and court rules, or any other legislative source.

  - Secondary source material, including examples or illustrations, explanations, or commentary about the law included in treatises, legal encyclopedias, dictionaries, or any other type of secondary legal materials.

  - Non-legal publications, including newspapers, video, the Internet, or any other source.

  - Facts or other information taken directly from court documents or filings.

- ✗ **Exception:** The *only* time you can refer to authority and skip a citation is when you are repeating a concept that you have previously discussed.

  - ☞ ***Example:*** The joint defense doctrine analyzed in <u>Smith</u> protects the statements our client made.

Caution

☞ If you omit a citation to primary authority, it tells the reader that there is <u>no authority</u> for what you just said, i.e., it's wishful thinking or argument, but not the law.

☞ If you use ideas or information from any type of authority, secondary source, or other publication without a citation, you run the risk of a plagiarism accusation. Don't tarnish your legal reputation, or ruin your career before it gets off the ground! When in doubt, ask your instructor or supervisor for guidance.

Examples: When to Cite

Michael Adams was employed by the National Bank of Detroit when he was mistakenly arrested and charged with making fraudulent withdrawals from the bank. [1] **Adams v. Nat'l Bank of Detroit, 508 N.W.2d 464, 464 (Mich. 1993).** The withdrawals were actually made by another NBD employee with the same last name. [2] **Id.** Adams suffered no physical injuries based on his arrest. [3] **Id.** The court held that Michigan law does not require that the plaintiff suffer a physical or mental injury to sustain an action for false imprisonment; an interference with a liberty interest is all that is required. [4] **Id. at 466.** Furthermore, any intent to confine the person is sufficient, and even an "innocent or reasonable mistake of identity" will not relieve the defendant from liability. [5] **Id.**	[1] Facts from a precedent case; citation is required.
	[2] Additional facts from the precedent case; citation is required. (Id. is a shortened form of citation.)
	[3] More facts from the precedent; citation is required.
	[4] Holding/rule stated; citation required.
	[5] Rule stated; citation required.
In our case, Mr. Smith's ten-hour detention interfered with his liberty interest. Although Mr. Smith suffered no physical or mental injuries when he was mistakenly detained by authorities on theft charges, as the court held in [6] **Adams**, no such injuries are required for a false imprisonment action. Lack of injuries will not relieve Shopper's Paradise of liability.	[6] Reference to authority previously discussed; no citation required when the writer, not the court, is applying or analyzing the law.

NOTE: Citations shown in this example are in bold and numbered for ease of reference. Do not put your citations in bold or number them.

D. Citation Sentences, Clauses, and Embedded Citations   Rule B1.1

One key difference between how academic writers cite in law review articles and practitioners cite in court documents lies in the placement of citations. Academic writers place citations in footnotes, while practitioners incorporate citations into the text directly after the propositions they support. Depending on the circumstances, this means the citation may be placed:

(a) In a separate **citation sentence** following a textual sentence (most common);

(b) Within a textual sentence in a separate **citation clause**, but only when the citation is not an integral part of the sentence itself; or

(c) **Embedded** within the textual sentence when the citation is integral to the meaning of the sentence.

The following two charts show examples of citation placement in practitioners' documents. Chart 1 shows citations to cases, while Chart 2 illustrates statutory citations. Look for differences in punctuation and abbreviations between citation sentences, clauses, and embedded citations. A detailed discussion of these differences follows the charts.

Chart 1: Case Citations

(a) Citation Sentence *The citations support the entire preceding sentence.*	(b) Citation Clause *The citations support only one part of the sentence.*	(c) Embedded Citation *The citations are an integral part of the sentence.*
Before a federally subsidized housing unit may be declared a drug haven, the Residential Drug-Related Evictions Act requires consideration of seven specified factors. **Cook v. Edgewood Mgmt. Corp., 825 A.2d 939, 946 (D.C. 2003).** Dismissal is inappropriate if, because of the presence of some of these factors, a jury could find a "legally sufficient evidentiary basis" for concluding that an apartment is a drug haven. **Railan v. Katyal, 766 A.2d 998, 1006 (D.C. 2001).**	Before a federally subsidized housing unit may be declared a drug haven, the court must consider seven specified factors, **Cook v. Edgewood Mgmt. Corp., 825 A.2d 939, 946 (D.C. 2003),** and dismissal is inappropriate if, because of the presence of some of these factors, a jury could find a "legally sufficient evidentiary basis" for concluding that an apartment is a drug haven, **Railan v. Katyal, 766 A.2d 998, 1006 (D.C. 2001).**	The court held in **Cook v. Edgewood Management Corp., 825 A.2d 939, 946 (D.C. 2003),** that before a federally subsidized housing unit may be declared a drug haven, the Residential Drug-Related Evictions Act requires consideration of seven specified factors. In the prior case of **Railan v. Katyal, 766 A.2d 998, 1006 (D.C. 2001),** dismissal was held to be inappropriate if, because of the presence of some of these factors, a jury could find a "legally sufficient evidentiary basis" for concluding that an apartment is a drug haven.

Chart 2: Statutory Citations

(a) Citation Sentence *The citations support the entire preceding sentence.*	(b) Citation Clause *The citations support only one part of the sentence.*	(c) Embedded Citation *The citations are an integral part of the sentence.*
The possession of a deadly weapon while committing a theft offense constitutes aggravated robbery. **Ohio Rev. Code Ann. § 2911.01 (West 2014).** Any instrument capable of inflicting death is classified as a deadly weapon. **§ 2923.11.**	The possession of a deadly weapon while committing a theft offense constitutes aggravated robbery, **Ohio Rev. Code Ann. § 2911.01 (West 2014),** and any instrument capable of inflicting death is classified as a deadly weapon, **§ 2923.11.**	According to **Ohio Revised Code Annotated section 2911.01 (West 2014),** the possession of a deadly weapon while committing a theft offense constitutes aggravated robbery. A deadly weapon is defined in **section 2923.11** as any instrument capable of inflicting death.

Distinguishing Between Citation Clauses and Embedded Citations

It is important to distinguish between citation clauses and embedded citations because different citation rules apply. What's the difference?

- In a **citation clause**, the citation itself is not essential (i.e., integral) to the meaning of the sentence. If the citation is stricken from the sentence, the sentence still makes sense.
- In an **embedded citation**, the citation itself is essential (i.e., integral) to the meaning of the sentence. If the citation is stricken from the sentence, the sentence no longer makes sense — something is obviously missing.

The examples below show how the meaning of the sentence is affected when the citations are stricken.

Citation Clause Citations are not *integral to the sentence.*	Embedded Citation Citations are *integral to the sentence.*
Probable cause exists if, under the totality of the circumstances, there is a fair probability that contraband will be found in a particular place, ~~Illinois v. Gates, 462 U.S. 213, 238 (1983),~~ but direct evidence is not required to obtain a search warrant ~~,~~ ~~United States v. Jones, 994 F.2d 1051, 1056 (3d Cir. 1993)~~.	According to the Supreme Court's holding in ~~Illinois v. Gates, 462 U.S. 213, 238 (1983),~~ probable cause exists if, under the totality of the circumstances, there is a fair probability that contraband will be found in a particular place, and the Third Circuit stated in ~~United States v. Jones, 994 F.2d 1051, 1056 (3d Cir. 1993)~~ that direct evidence is not required to obtain a search warrant.

☞ To avoid awkward citations, rewrite sentences containing embedded citations so that the citation is placed in a citation sentence at the end of the text sentence.

1. Citation Sentences

Citation sentences are the most common and preferred method of citation.

- **Basic Rule:** When the citation supports the entire sentence, place the citation after the text sentence. The citation sentence begins with a capital letter and has a period at its end—it is its own complete sentence.

Examples: Citation Sentences

Case Citation	Repetition of the same proposition in several jury instructions is generally within the discretion of the trial court and is not reversible error. **Wood v. Hulsey, 271 S.W.2d 218, 222 (Mo. Ct. App. 1954).**
Statutory Citation	Virginia's DUI statute makes it unlawful for a person to drive any motor vehicle while under the influence of alcohol. **Va. Code Ann. § 18.2-266 (2019).**

2. Citation Clauses

Citation clauses are most commonly used when a single sentence is supported by two or more authorities; see the first two examples, below. Occasionally citation clauses are used when one part of the sentence is from an authority, and another part is the application of the authority; see the third example in the chart below.

- **Basic Rule:** When the citation supports only part of the textual sentence, AND the authority is NOT an integral part of the sentence, set the citation off from the textual sentence with commas.

Examples: Citation Clauses

Statute and Case In Single Sentence	Using litigation reports concerning accidents caused by the failure of a locomotive boiler is statutorily barred, **49 U.S.C. § 20703 (2012),** revealing an explicit Congressional policy to rule out reports of accidents even though they may have a claim to objectivity, **Palmer v. Hoffman, 318 U.S. 109, 115 (1943).**
Two Cases In Single Sentence	Exigent circumstances permit a warrantless seizure without probable cause to believe that a crime has been committed, **Figg v. Schroeder, 312 F.3d 625, 639 (4th Cir. 2002),** and such circumstances exist when police officers engaged in lawful investigatory functions would be endangered unless they conducted a warrantless seizure, **Michigan v. Summers, 452 U.S. 692, 702–03 (1981).**

Examples: Citation Clauses, *continued*

One Case Supporting First Part of Sentence Only	Although in Virginia the tort of false imprisonment requires the "direct restraint" of physical liberty, **Jordan v. Shands, 500 S.E.2d 215, 218 (Va. 1998),** we do not get to the issue of restraint in our case because there was adequate legal justification.

Avoiding Awkward Citation Placement: Part 1

Including multiple citations can lead to long, awkwardly constructed, and difficult to follow sentences. When possible, divide single sentences with multiple citations into separate sentences containing one citation each.

First example from previous page, rewritten:

> Using litigation reports concerning accidents resulting from the failure of a locomotive boiler is statutorily barred. **49 U.S.C. § 20703 (2018).** This reveals an explicit Congressional policy to rule out reports of accidents even though they may have a claim to objectivity. **Palmer v. Hoffman, 318 U.S. 109, 115 (1943).**

---

3. Embedded Citations   Rule 10.1.1(vi)

- **Basic Rule: Case Citations.** When a case citation is embedded into the textual sentence and forms an integral part of the sentence, provide the citation followed by a comma. Do not place a comma before the citation.

- **Basic Rule: Other Authorities.** When an authority other than a case is embedded into a textual sentence, include the citation without a following comma unless the citation is at the end of an introductory phrase or independent clause that would ordinarily require a comma.

Examples: Embedded Citations

Embedded Citation: Case	The court stated in **Stamathis v. Flying J, Inc., 389 F.3d 429, 441 (4th Cir. 2004),** that the lack of probable cause alone does not infer actual malice but does lend support to that finding.
Embedded Citation: Other Authority	Robbery is defined by **North Dakota Century Code section 12.1-22-01 (2014)** as a theft accompanied by the infliction or attempted infliction of bodily injury upon another.

Chart continues on the next page.

Examples: Embedded Citations, *continued*

Embedded Citation: Independent Clause	According to **Minnesota Statutes section 146B.03 (2016),** all persons performing tattooing must hold a valid tattoo technician license.

Avoiding Awkward Citation Placement: Part 2

Embedding a citation in a text sentence interrupts the narrative flow and lessens the impact of the point you are making. This is especially true if the citation is toward the beginning of the sentence. Whenever possible, rewrite the sentence to place the citation in a separate citation sentence.

Rewritten example from previous page:

> While the lack of probable cause alone does not infer actual malice, it does lend support to that finding. Stamathis v. Flying J, Inc., 389 F.3d 429, 441 (4th Cir. 2004).

Splitting Full Case Citations

A split case citation is one where the case name appears in the text of the sentence but the remainder appears in a citation sentence at the end. Split citations are used by academic writers, but are not "approved" for practitioners.

☞ Local practice in some areas allows split citations even in practitioners' documents. Before using, ask your instructor or supervisor if splitting full citations is acceptable. When using a split citation keep in mind that they can only be used when there is **one** citation in the sentence, and never with citation clauses.

Most sentences can be revised to eliminate the need for the case name in the text, eliminating the need for a split citation, as shown in the example below.

With Split Citation	Without Split Citation
The court held in **Wood v. Hulsey** that repetition of the same proposition in several jury instructions is generally within the discretion of the trial court and is not reversible error. **271 S.W.2d 218, 222 (Mo. Ct. App. 1954).**	Repetition of the same proposition in several jury instructions is generally within the discretion of the trial court and is not reversible error. **Wood v. Hulsey, 271 S.W.2d 218, 222 (Mo. Ct. App. 1954).**

☞ A type of split citation can be used with *short form* case citations. See discussion in Chapter 2, on page 55.

E. Pinpoint Citations   Rule 3

One purpose of legal citation is to provide the reader with the information necessary to locate the cited authority, and the exact place in that authority where the cited material can be found. That exact place is called a pinpoint or pincite. Except when referring to an authority in general, provide the specific page, section or paragraph number, footnote, or supplement, where the cited material appears.

The method used to pinpoint depends upon the specific authority cited and is covered in detail in the chapters on those authorities. This section introduces the general rules for pinpoint citation that are applicable to multiple types of authorities including:

1. **Pages:** One or multiple pages of a case, book, article, or other paginated authority, beginning on page 18.

2. **Sections:** One or multiple sections or subsections of a statute, treatise, or other authority divided into sections, beginning on page 19.

3. **Paragraphs:** One or multiple paragraphs or subparagraphs of material divided into numbered paragraphs, beginning on page 21.

4. **Lines:** One or multiple lines of paginated material, beginning on page 21.

5. **Footnotes:** One or multiple footnotes, beginning on page 22.

6. **Endnotes:** One or multiple endnotes, beginning on page 23.

7. **Supplements:** Material appearing in a pocket part or supplement, beginning on page 24.

☞ For information on pinpointing other types of subdivisions (tables, graphs, appendices, etc.) see *Bluebook* Rule 3.

About Hyphens and En Dashes

Hyphens are a type of punctuation occurring frequently in citations, especially statutes. An **en dash** is another punctuation mark used to separate consecutive pages or section numbers in pinpoints. Another type of dash—called an **em dash**—is used to set off text (as in this sentence), but is not used in citation. What's the difference?

A **hyphen** is short dash mark:	-
An **en dash** is a wider dash mark:	–
An **em dash** is an even wider dash mark:	—

Most *Bluebook* rules allow you to use hyphens or en dashes interchangeably, but in certain situations using the wider en dash is preferred. Look for hints on when to use hyphens or en dashes throughout this guide.

☞ This guide uses **en dashes** to separate consecutive pages or section numbers.

Box continues on the next page.

☞ To create an en dash, insert a special character or symbol from the drop down menu.

☞ Your word processing program may be set to default to an en dash when you type two hyphens in succession. Check it and see.

---

1. Pages   Rule 3.2(a)

- **Basic Rule No. 1: Single Page.** For an authority divided into pages, provide the exact page number where the cited material can be found.

- **Basic Rule No. 2: Multiple Consecutive Pages.** To cite material spanning two or more consecutive pages, give the inclusive page numbers, separated by an en dash or hyphen. Retain the last TWO digits, but drop other repetitious digits.

  Example: 662–63   *Not:* 662–663

- **Basic Rule No. 3: Multiple Nonconsecutive Pages.** To cite material that appears on two or more nonconsecutive pages (i.e., skips pages), give the pinpoint page numbers separated by a comma. Retain all digits, even if repetitious.

  Example: 414, 418   *Not:* 414, 18

- **Basic Rule No. 4: First Page.** To cite material that appears on the first page of a paginated authority (e.g., cases, periodicals), repeat the page number as the pinpoint. Do not omit the pinpoint even though it is repetitive.

  Example: 467 S.W.2d **363, 363**

Examples: Citing Pages

Basic Rule No.	Examples
No. 1 **Single Page**	Rice v. Collins, 546 U.S. 333, **341** (2006). Douglas Hay et al., Albion's Fatal Tree **43** (1975).
No. 2 **Multiple Consecutive Pages**	United States v. Pineyro, 112 F.3d 43, **45–46** (2d Cir. 1997). Paul E. Lund, National Banks and Diversity Jurisdiction, 46 U. Louisville L. Rev. 73, **105–06** (2007). Id. at **104–05**. State v. Kwak, 909 P.2d 1106, **1111–12** (Haw. 1995). Short v. United States, 50 F.3d 994, **999–1000** (Fed. Cir. 1995). ☞ Notice that the page numbers in the range pinpointed in this last example are not repetitious, so both numbers are included in full.

Chart continues on the next page.

Examples: Citing Pages, *continued*

Basic Rule No.	Examples
No. 3 **Multiple Non-Consecutive Pages**	<u>Id.</u> at **103, 105**. State v. Kwak, 909 P.2d 1106, **1110, 1112** (Haw. 1995). Lund, <u>supra</u>, at **103, 106**. Paggett v. Kroger Co., 719 S.E.2d 792, **793, 795** (Ga. Ct. App. 2011).
No. 4 **First Page**	<u>United States v. Pineyro</u>, 112 F.3d **43, 43** (2d Cir. 1997). Paul E. Lund, <u>National Banks and Diversity Jurisdiction</u>, 46 U. Louisville L. Rev. **73, 73** (2007).

2. Sections and Subsections   Rule 3.3

Follow the rules below to pinpoint one or more sections or subsections of a statute, book, or other authority divided into sections.

☞ To create a section symbol, see the discussion of symbols on page 152 of this guide.

☞ Always include a **space** between the section symbol and section number.

☞ Section numbers may include punctuation in the form of a periods, colons, or hyphens. Be sure to use the correct punctuation—they are not interchangeable.

☞ Use an **en dash** to separate multiple consecutive sections or subsections. Although *The Bluebook* allows either an en dash or hyphen, the wider en dash should be used to distinguish multiple sections from ordinary punctuation included in the section number. See "**About Hyphens and En Dashes**" on page 17 of this guide.

● Basic Rule No. 1: Single Section. Include a section symbol followed by the section number where the specific material is found.

   Examples: § 1874   § 284.15   § 68:29   § 320-45-16

● Basic Rule No. 2: Consecutive Sections. To pinpoint material spanning two or more consecutive sections, provide the section numbers, separated by an en dash. Use TWO section symbols to indicate multiple sections. If the second section number contains repetitious digits, follow the rules below based on the punctuation within the section numbers.

   (a) *No punctuation:* If the section numbers contain no punctuation, retain all digits of the section number, even if repetitious. Do not include spaces before or after the en dash.

   Examples: §§ 1874–1875   §§ 395–398

(b) *Period or colon:* If the section numbers are punctuated with periods or colons, omit repetitious digits preceding the final punctuation. Separate the sections using an **en dash**, then include the punctuation and the non-repetitive digits. Do not include spaces before or after the en dash.

Examples: §§ 284.15–.16   §§ 68:29–:30

(c) *Hyphen:* If the section numbers are punctuated with hyphens, omit repetitious digits preceding the final punctuation. Include the word "to" before the punctuation (hyphen) and the non-repetitious digits. Include spaces before and after "to."

Examples: §§ 320-45-16 **to** -17   ***Not:***   §§ 320-45-16–17.

- **Basic Rule No. 3: Non-Consecutive Sections.** To cite material that skips sections (non-consecutive sections) *within one title or chapter,* provide the section numbers separated by a comma. Use TWO section symbols to indicate multiple sections. If the section number contains no punctuation, retain all digits of the section number, even if repetitious. If the section number contains punctuation, omit repetitious digits preceding the punctuation, unless the result would be ambiguous.

Examples: §§ 1874, 1877   §§ 284.15, .18   §§ 68:29, :34   §§ 320-45-16, -22

Sections are frequently broken down into smaller subdivisions, called subsections, sub-subsections, etc. Always pinpoint to the narrowest subdivision possible.

- **Basic Rule No. 4: Single Subsection.** To cite material located in a subsection, provide the section number as described in Basic Rule No. 1 for Sections. Append the subsection letter or number immediately after the section number, without spaces before or after, and place the subsection in parentheses.

Examples: § 1874(b)   § 284.15(1)   § 68:29(G)   § 320-45-16(a)

- **Basic Rule No. 5: Single Sub-Subsection.** To cite material located in a sub-subsection, follow Basic Rule No. 4 for Single Subsections. Append the sub-subsection letter or number immediately after the subsection letter or number, without spaces before or after, and placing the sub-subsection in parentheses. Repeat for any additional subdivisions, appending each to the end of the previous subdivision, without spaces, and placing each in parentheses.

Examples: § 1874(b)(2)   § 284.15(1)(a)   § 68:29(G)(1)(c)   § 320-45-16(a)(3)(B)(iii)

- **Basic Rule No. 6: Consecutive Subsections.** To cite material spanning two or more consecutive subsections (or sub-subsections) of a single section, provide the subsection numbers, separated by an en dash (preferred) or hyphen. Use ONE section symbol (because you are citing only one *section*).

Examples: § 1874(b)–(c)   § 284.15(1)–(3)   § 68:29(G)(1)(c)–(e)

- Basic Rule No. 7: Non-Consecutive Subsections. To cite material that skips subsections (non-consecutive subsections) of a single section, provide the subsection numbers separated by a comma. Use ONE section symbol (because you are citing only one *section*). Include a space after the comma.

  Examples: § 1874(b), (f)   § 284.15(1), (4)   § 68:29(G)(1)(c), (g)

3. Paragraphs   Rule 3.3

Paragraphs are cited exactly like sections. Follow the rules for sections, above, substituting the paragraph symbol for the section symbol.

☞ To create a paragraph symbol, see the discussion of symbols on page 152 of this guide.

☞ Always include a **space** between the paragraph symbol and paragraph number.

Examples: Pinpointing Paragraphs

Single Paragraph	¶ 29
Consecutive Paragraphs	¶¶ 42–43
Non-Consecutive Paragraphs	¶¶ 15, 22
Paragraph with Subparagraphs	¶ 29(b)
Paragraph with Multiple Consecutive Subparagraphs	¶ 18(a)–(c)
Paragraph with Multiple Non-Consecutive Subparagraphs	¶ 37(d), (f)

4. Lines   Rule B17.1.2

Many litigation documents, and a few other sources, divide material into lines. If the source has numbered lines, pinpoint to the precise line numbers.

- Basic Rule No. 1: Single Line. Include the page number where the material appears, followed by a colon and the line number.

  Examples: 15:25   2:12

- Basic Rule No. 2: Multiple Consecutive Lines. To cite material spanning two or more consecutive lines:

  (a) If the lines appear on a **single page**, include the page number, a colon, the beginning line number followed by an en dash (preferred) or hyphen, and the ending line number.

  Examples: 15:25–28   2:12–18

  (b) If the lines are on **consecutive pages**, provide the beginning page number, a colon, the beginning line number followed by an en dash (preferred) or hyphen, the ending page number followed by a colon and the ending line number.

  Examples: 15:25–16:3   2:12–3:11

- Basic Rule No. 3: Multiple Non-Consecutive Lines. Cite as shown for multiple *consecutive* lines, but substitute a comma for the en dash.

Examples: Multiple Non-Consecutive Lines

All lines on same page	15:25, 28 2:12, 18
Lines on different pages	15:25, 18:3 2:12, 3:11

5. Footnotes   Rule 3.2(b)

- Basic Rule No. 1: Single Footnote. If the cited material appears in a footnote, cite the page, section, or paragraph number of the text where the footnote reference appears, followed by the abbreviation "n." and the footnote number.

  ☞ There is no space between the "n." and the footnote number.

- Basic Rule No. 2: Page and Footnote. To cite material appearing in *both* the text *and* in the footnote, include the page, section or paragraph number of the text where the material is found, followed by an **ampersand** (&), the "n." abbreviation for footnote, and the footnote number.

- Basic Rule No. 3: Consecutive Footnotes. To cite material spanning two or more consecutive footnotes, give the inclusive note numbers, separated by an en dash or hyphen. Use TWO note number abbreviations (nn.) to indicate multiple footnotes. Retain the last TWO digits, but drop other repetitious digits.

- Basic Rule No. 4: Non-Consecutive Footnotes. To cite material that appears in two or more non-consecutive footnotes (i.e., skips footnotes) on the same page, give the note numbers separated by an ampersand. Use TWO note abbreviations (nn.) to indicate multiple footnotes. Retain all digits, even if repetitious. When footnotes appear on different pages, cite pages individually.

Examples: Pinpointing Footnotes

Basic Rule No.	Examples
No. 1 **Single Footnote**	Abrishamian v. Barbely, 981 A.2d 797, 802 **n.4** (Md. Ct. Spec. App. 2009). Daniel L. Brenner, Creating Effective Broadband Network Regulation, 62 Fed. Comm. L.J. 13, 23 **n.41** (2010).
No. 2 **Page and** **Footnote**	Abdul-Kabir v. Quarterman, 550 U.S. 233, **259 & n.21** (2007).
No. 3 **Consecutive** **Footnotes**	Langley v. DaimlerChrysler Corp., 502 F.3d 475, 482 **nn.2–3** (6th Cir. 2007).
No. 4 **Non-Consecu-** **tive Footnotes**	Billings v. Aeropres Corp., 522 F. Supp. 2d 1121, 1124 **nn.10 & 12** (E.D. Ark. 2007). Id. at 1126 nn.21 & 23, 27 nn.33 & 37.

6. Endnotes   Rule 3.2(c)

- Basic Rule No. 1: Single Endnote. If the cited material appears in an endnote, cite the page *where the endnote actually appears*, not the page in the text that refers to the endnote. Follow with the abbreviation "n." and the endnote number. There is no space between the "n." and the endnote number.

- Basic Rule No. 2: Page and Endnote. To cite material appearing in *both* the text *and* in the endnote, include the page number of the text where the material is found, followed by an **ampersand** (&), the page number where the endnote appears, the "n." abbreviation for endnote, and the endnote number.

☞ To cite material appearing in multiple endnotes, follow the guidelines for footnotes, above.

Examples: Endnotes

Basic Rule No.	Examples
No. 1 **Single Endnote**	Wallace P. Mullin et al., <u>Should Firms Be Allowed to Indemnify Their Employees for Sanctions?</u>, 26 J.L. Econ. & Org. 30, **53 n.3** (2010).
No. 2 **Page & Endnote**	Wallace P. Mullin et al., <u>Should Firms Be Allowed to Indemnify Their Employees for Sanctions?</u>, 26 J.L. Econ. & Org. 30, **38 & 53 n.3** (2010).

7. Supplements   Rule 3.1(c)

- **Basic Rule:** To indicate the material appears in a pocket part or supplement to the main volume, include the abbreviation "Supp." in the end parenthetical. Pinpoint to the page or section number of the supplement.

☞ To cite material found in both the main volume AND in the supplement, see *Bluebook* Rule 3.1(c).

Examples: Supplements

Statute	Wash. Rev. Code § 61.24.040 (**Supp.** 2015).
Treatise	Arne Werchick, <u>Civil Jury Selection</u> § 12.6 (2d ed. **Supp.** 2014).

F. Spacing Rules for Citation Abbreviations   Rule 6.1

The Bluebook has detailed rules for when to insert blank spaces in a citation. ALWAYS pay very close attention to the spacing in *The Bluebook* examples, and ALWAYS ignore the spacing shown in the original authority.

- **Basic Rule No. 1:** Always put a space between each word and distinct part of the citation. In the following examples • indicates a required space.

  ☞ Metzler•v.•Rowell,•547•S.E.2d•311,•314•(Ga.•Ct.•App.•2001).

  ☞ Ohio•Rev.•Code•Ann.•§•2911.01•(West•2019).

  ☞ Jamal•Greene,•Note,•Judging•Partisan•Gerrymanders•Under•the•Elections•Clause,•114•Yale•L.J.•1021,•1044•(2005).

- Basic Rule No. 2: **The Adjacent Single Capitals Rule.** In abbreviations, DO NOT use spaces when the abbreviation consists of "adjacent single capitals," i.e., a single capital letter followed by another single capital letter. *Bluebook* Rule 6.1(a).

  ☞ Numerals and ordinals in citations (2d, 3d, 4th, 5th, etc.) are treated as single-letter abbreviations for the purposes of this rule.

✗ **Exception 1:** Periodical Citations. When citing a periodical, insert a space between single adjacent capitals making up the institution's name, and capitals that are part of the publication's title. See discussion of periodicals in Chapter 7 of this guide, page 103.

✗ **Exception 2:** Court Documents. When briefs and other documents filed in courts are subject to word limits, spacing in the source segment of the citation may be "closed up." See discussion in Chapter 2 of this guide, page 35.

Examples: Single Adjacent Capitals Rule 6.1(a)

Adjacent Single Capital Letters	Mixed Single and Multiple-Letter Abbreviations
S.D.N.Y. 4 single adjacent capitals.	**S. Ct.** 1 capital, adjacent to 2-letter abbreviation.
S.E.2d 2 adjacent single capitals + 1 adjacent ordinal.	**Mass. App. Ct.** 4 letter abbreviation + 3 letters + 2 letters.
P.3d 1 single capital + 1 adjacent ordinal.	**So. 2d** 2 letter abbreviation, adjacent to 1 ordinal.
U.S.C. 3 single adjacent capitals.	**F. Supp. 2d** 1 capital, adjacent to 4-letter abbreviation, adjacent to ordinal.
J.K. v. R.K.M. 2 and 3 single adjacent capitals.	**F.G. Jones, Inc.** 2 single capitals adjacent to 5-letter word.

G. Introduction to Short Form Citations   Rule 4

Full citations contain all the information a reader may need to determine the source of the cited material. Depending on the specific source cited, full citations can be long and cumbersome. As a partial solution, *The Bluebook* allows the use of shortened citation forms for repeated references to the same authority. This section discusses the most common short forms used by practitioners:

1. <u>Id.</u>, used with any type of authority, discussed on this page;

2. <u>Supra</u>, used for some secondary sources, discussed on page 27; and

3. Alternate short form, for situations where <u>id.</u> or <u>supra</u> cannot be used. Alternate short forms vary depending upon the source or authority being cited, and are discussed in the chapters for the specific authority.

Additional information on how to use short forms with a specific type of authority is found in the chapter for the individual authority.

- **Basic Rule:** Once a full citation has been given, a shortened form may be used for subsequent citations to the *same* authority found within the *same general discussion*. Short forms are one of the three types discussed below.

☞ Local custom may vary with respect to the meaning of "same general discussion." Seek advice from your instructor or supervisor.

1. <u>Id.</u>   Rule 4.1

<u>Id.</u> is the abbreviation for the Latin word *idem*, which means "the same." It is used to indicate that the immediately preceding citation is to the same authority. If there has been an intervening citation to different authority between the current citation and the previous mention of the same authority, <u>id.</u> cannot be used and an alternate short form must be used instead.

- **Basic Rule No. 1: All <u>Id.</u> Short Forms.** Use <u>id.</u> to cite the **same** authority as was cited in the **immediately preceding** citation, observing the following rules:

  - <u>Id.</u> is always ♦ underlined or italicized.

  - Use <u>id.</u> only with citation sentences and clauses; do not use in embedded citations.

  - <u>Id.</u> is capitalized when it starts a citation sentence, but use a lower case <u>id.</u> in citation clauses.

- **Basic Rule No. 2: Pinpointing Same Page or Section.** When the cited material is found on the same page or in the same section as the immediately preceding citation, no pinpoint is required.

- **Basic Rule No. 3: Pinpointing Different Page or Section.** When the cited material is found on a different page or in a different section than the immediately preceding citation, include a pinpoint. Follow the appropriate rule below:

  (a) **Pages:** Include the word "at" and the new page number.

  > ***Examples:*** Id. at 578. ***or*** *Id.* at 578.

  (b) **Sections:** Include a section symbol [§] and the new section number.

  > ***Examples:*** Id. § 166(a) ***or*** *Id.* § 166(a).

  (c) **Subsections:** Include a section symbol [§], the section number, and the new subsection number. Do not include only the new section number.

  > ***Examples:*** Id. § 166(f) ***or*** *Id.* § 166(f) ☞ **Not:** Id. § (f).

☞ Id. can be used in citation sentences and clauses, but **not** in embedded citations, nor as a substitute for the case name in a text sentence.

> ***Right:*** In deciding Armstrong the court looked at several competing factors.
>
> ***Wrong:*** In deciding id. the court looked at several competing factors.

2. Supra   Rule 4.2

Supra is a Latin word meaning "above." It is the short form used to refer the reader to a previous part of a document where the full citation is found. It is used for some types of *secondary* authorities after an intervening citation to different authority.

- **Basic Rule:** Use supra when id. cannot be used because of an intervening citation to different authority. When the use of supra is appropriate, include the following in the citation:

  (1) The author's name, followed by a comma;

  (2) The word supra, ♦ underlined or italicized, followed by a comma;

  (3) The word "at" if citing pages, or a section symbol if citing sections; and

  (4) A pinpoint citation to the page or section number.

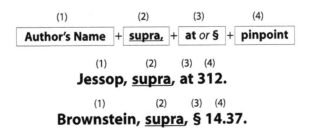

☞ See *Bluebook* Rule 4.2 for a list of publications where <u>supra</u> is appropriate, and check the Bluepages for examples of <u>supra</u> citations for individual publications.

☞ <u>Supra</u> is NEVER used as a short form for cases, statutes, constitutions, court rules, or regulations.

3. Alternate Short Forms

Individual authorities, including cases, statutes, and constitutions, have special rules for short form citations when <u>id.</u> cannot be used. These special short forms are discussed in the chapters pertaining to the specific authority.

2 Cases

Bluebook Whitepages Rule 10, Bluepages Rule B10, and Table 1 control the form for case citations.

Case citations are not mysterious—they are simply an assemblage of component parts following a few specific rules for each segment.

Court decisions are available from a number of sources, including print and electronic sources. This chapter addresses citation forms for cases obtained from **print** sources. Cases obtained from **electronic sources** (commercial databases or the Internet) are discussed in Chapter 13.

Included in this chapter are discussions of:

A. The basic rules for case citations, beginning on page 30;

B. Special rules for case names, beginning on page 40;

C. Short form citations, beginning on page 52;

D. Parallel citations, beginning on page 58;

E. Public domain (format neutral) citations, beginning on page 59;

F. Parenthetical information, including dissents and concurrences, citing and quoting parentheticals, and weight of authority, beginning on page 62;

G. Subsequent history, beginning on page 65; and

H. The ordering of multiple parentheticals, beginning on page 66.

Caution

☞ **NEVER** rely on the source itself to provide the correct citation form. The major publishers, print and electronic, use their own citation styles that at times differ significantly from *Bluebook* style. **ALWAYS** conform your citations to *The Bluebook*.

A. Basic Case Citation Rules   Rules 10, B10 & Table 1

Every published opinion begins with a case caption containing the information needed for a full citation to the case. The caption also contains information that is *not* used in a citation. Details of each segment of the citation, including what information to include and what information to omit, are contained in the next few pages of this guide.

- **Basic Rule: Full Case Citations.** The first time a case is cited in a document, prepare a full citation by providing the following information:

  (1) Case name, followed by a comma;

  (2) Source information including the:

      (a) volume;

      (b) reporter name, including any series number, abbreviated;

      (c) beginning page number; and

      (d) pinpoint page number, if applicable;

  (3) Court information, identifying the court rendering the decision; and

  (4) Year of the decision.

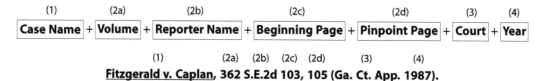

Before constructing the citation, determine whether the citation will appear in a citation sentence or clause, or will be embedded in the textual sentence—the rules may be different depending on where the citation appears. See discussion of citation sentences, clauses, and embedded citations beginning on page 14 of this guide.

1. Case Name   Rules 10.2.1, 10.2.2, B10.1.1

A full citation to a case begins with the case name. There are *many* rules that control case names in citations. To get you started, this section focuses on the simplest form: individuals suing other individuals. Other types of parties such as businesses, governmental departments, and situations where additional information is included in the caption such as descriptive terms or procedural phrases, are discussed in Part B of this chapter beginning on page 40. For a list of these special situations, see "More on Case Names," on page 32.

(1)

| Case Name | + | Volume | + | Reporter Name | + | Beginning Page | + | Pinpoint Page | + | Court | + | Year |

(1)
Fitzgerald v. Caplan, 362 S.E.2d 103, 105 (Ga. Ct. App. 1987).

- **Basic Rule No. 1: Individuals.** Provide the names of the parties to the action in the order they are shown in the caption. Include only the surname (last name). For hyphenated surnames, include both names. Separate the parties' names with a "v."; do not spell out versus or abbreviate to "vs." In addition, omit the following:
  - First and middle names or initials;
  - Designations such as Jr., Sr., or IV;
  - Professional or courtesy titles such as Prof., Dr., Sgt., Mr./Mrs./Ms.; and
  - Designations such as plaintiff, appellant, etc., that follow the name.

♦ <u>Underline</u> or *italicize* the entire case name, but NOT the comma that follows the case name.

   Examples:

Susan G. Tree v. Sherry B. Jones	☞	<u>Tree v. Jones</u>
Jeffrey Wohl, **Jr.** v. Albert Biggins, **M.D.**	☞	<u>Wohl v. Biggins</u>
Carl Rasul-Morgan v. Cynthia Albi-Kahn	☞	<u>Rasul-Morgan v. Albi-Kahn</u>

✗ **Exception 1:** If a party's name consists of initials only, or a first name and last initial, include the initials in the citations. Close up single adjacent capital letters; see discussion on page 24 of this guide.

   Examples:

   | C. J. v. L. M. | ☞ | <u>C.J. v. L.M.</u> |
   | Jasmine D. v. City of Davis | ☞ | <u>Jasmine D. v. City of Davis</u> |

✗ **Exception 2:** If a party's name is in a language where the surname (last name) is given first, as in many Asian names, include the full name.

   Example:

   | Fong Yue Ting v. United States | ☞ | <u>Fong Yue Ting v. United States</u> |

   ☞ If a party's name is of Portugese or Spanish origin and includes multiple surnames, see *Bluebook* Rule 10.2.1(g).

- **Basic Rule No. 2: Multiple Parties.** Many cases have multiple appellants, appellees, or both, listed in the caption. Include only the **first-named** party for each side of the action.

   Example:

   | Henry Armstrong **and** Janet Craig versus Marjorie Dixon **and** John Earley | ☞ | <u>Armstrong v. Dixon</u> |

- **Basic Rule No. 3: Et Al.** Some captions indicate additional parties by including the term "**et al.**" (a Latin abbreviation indicating there are additional parties), "**et ux.**" (Latin abbreviation for "and wife"), or "**etc.**" Always omit et al., et ux., etc., or similar terms from the case name.

    Example:

    Henry Armstrong **et ux.**
    versus   ☞   <u>Armstrong v. Dixon</u>
    Marjorie Dixon **et al.**

- **Basic Rule No. 4: Multiple Actions.** Occasionally a case will list multiple *actions*, perhaps because a cross-complaint was filed against a third party, or two or more cases have been consolidated into a single action. Include only the **first action** listed.

☞ You will know when this situation arises if there is more than one "versus" in the caption.

    Example:

    Henry Armstrong
    versus
    Marjorie Dixon   ☞   <u>Armstrong v. Dixon</u>
    versus
    Travelers Insurance, Cross-Complainant

More on Case Names

You will frequently encounter situations where the party is not an individual or additional information is appended to the case name. These situations are subject to special *Bluebook* rules. The following list includes the most commonly encountered case names where special rules apply. Each situation is discussed in detail in Part B of this Chapter, beginning on the page indicated.

- Businesses, organizations, or other non-governmental entities, page 40;
- Governmental bodies and their departments and agencies, including the United States, individual states, counties, and cities, page 42;
- Alternate names, including a/k/a, d/b/a, etc., page 47;
- Procedural terms and phrases, including estate of, in re, etc., or situations where there is no adversarial party, page 47;
- Descriptive terms and phrases, including trustee, warden, secretary, etc., page 47;
- Unions, page 51; and
- Internal Revenue Service Commissioner, page 52.

2. Source Information   Rules 10.3, B10.1.2 & Table 1

Opinions issued by courts are available from multiple sources, including sets of print volumes, commercial databases maintained by legal publishers, websites maintained by courts, and on hundreds of Internet websites. This Chapter discusses only print sources. Citation forms for online sources are discussed in Chapter 13.

The same case may be published in more than one set of print reporters. For example, many states publish their opinions in both a state reporter and a regional reporter. Modern United States Supreme Court decisions are published in three reporters and the United States Law Week, while older opinions are published under a variety of publications named after the person holding the office of Reporter of Decisions.

☞ Lists of all available print reporters for each jurisdiction are found in *Bluebook* Table 1. Federal jurisdictions (Supreme Court, circuit courts, district courts, etc.) are listed in Table 1.1, and state courts are listed alphabetically in Table 1.3.

When multiple reporters are listed in the case caption, cite to only **one source**. *Bluebook* Tables 1.1 (federal) and 1.3 (states) designate the "correct" reporter to cite for each jurisdiction. Use the explanation below to choose the correct reporter to cite.

☞ **Parallel Citations:** If local rules require citations to two or more reporters, see page 58 of this guide.

☞ **Public Domain Citations:** If local rules require the use of public domain citations, also known as medium-neutral format, see page 59 of this guide.

• **Basic Rule: Source Information.** In a full citation, include the following information about the source of the opinion. Each part is discussed in detail, below.

(a) The volume number;

(b) The abbreviated name of the reporter set, including series number, if any;

(c) The beginning page number; and

(d) The pinpoint page number (in most situations).

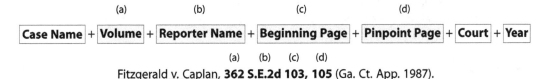

```
        (a)           (b)            (c)              (d)
Case Name + Volume + Reporter Name + Beginning Page + Pinpoint Page + Court + Year
             (a)  (b)   (c)   (d)
Fitzgerald v. Caplan, 362 S.E.2d 103, 105 (Ga. Ct. App. 1987).
```

Determining the "Correct" Reporter to Cite

1. Find the jurisdiction in *Bluebook* Table 1.1 (federal) or 1.3 (states).

2. Find the entry for the court you will cite (e.g., Supreme, Appellate, District, etc.).

3. Read the blurb immediately following the court heading. It will say "cite to [reporter name], if therein." Some entries add "otherwise cite to [reporter name]." Underneath that main heading one or several reporters are listed with the full name, coverage dates, and abbreviation.

4. The "correct" reporter to cite is the first-named reporter (look for the words "if therein"). The alternate reporter set is cited ONLY if the case does not appear in the first-named reporter.

☞ For state court cases, *The Bluebook* always lists the regional reporter as the first choice. However, local rules may require practitioners to cite their own state's reporters instead. Check the local rules, or ask your instructor or supervisor.

Example: Citing an Illinois Appellate Court Decision

1. The case caption printed at the right shows the case is published in three reporters: Illinois Appellate Court Reports, North Eastern Reporter, and West's Illinois Decisions.

2. Find **Illinois** in Table 1.3, then find the court you wish to cite (it is the second group in Table 1.3, labeled **Appellate Court**).

3. Read the blurb immediately following the court heading: **"Cite to N.E.2d or N.E.3d, if therein."**

4. The correct reporter to cite is, according to the T1.3 entry, the North Eastern Reporter. The citation for this example is: <u>People v. Walls</u>, **806 N.E.2d** 712 (Ill. App. Ct. 2004).

> THE PEOPLE OF THE STATE OF ILLINOIS
> v.
> MICHAEL A. WALLS
>
> APPELLATE COURT OF ILLINOIS,
> FIFTH DISTRICT
>
> 346 Ill. App. 3d 1154
> **806 N.E.2d 712**
> 282 Ill. Dec. 415
>
> March 19, 2004

☞ Many reporter sets are published in "series." For example, the North Eastern Reporter is published in three series: (1) North Eastern Reporter [abbreviated N.E.]; (2) North Eastern Reporter, Second Series [abbreviated N.E.2d]; and (3) North Eastern Reporter, Third Series [abbreviated N.E.3d]. Be sure to cite the correct series.

☞ Compare the Illinois entry in Table 1.3 to the Colorado Court of Appeals entry. The Colorado entry lists several possible reporters you can cite, but the "correct" reporter is the Pacific Reporter (abbreviated P., P.2d, or P.3d).

☞ Both Illinois and Colorado have adopted a public domain citation format for recent cases. The 2004 Illinois case used as an example here is not subject to the public domain rules. For additional information on public domain citations, see page 59 of this guide.

(a) Volume

- **Basic Rule:** Provide the volume number of the reporter set where the case appears.

(b) Reporter Name   Rules 10.3.2, B10.1.2, Table 1

- **Basic Rule:** Include the name of the "correct" reporter, abbreviated as shown in Table 1. Include the series number, if any, also abbreviated as shown in Table 1.

  ☞ Be sure to carefully copy the abbreviations and spacing shown in Table 1. For assistance with spacing, see the discussion on page 24 of this guide.

- ✗ **Exception: Court Documents.** In briefs or other documents submitted to courts, abbreviations in reporter names may be closed up to conserve space. Use this option only when the receiving court imposes word limits. See Bluepages rule B6.

  ### Examples:

  | F. Supp. 3d | *becomes* | F.Supp.3d |
  | Cal. Rptr. 2d | *becomes* | Cal.Rptr.2d |

  ☞ This is a new rule with the latest edition of *The Bluebook*. Because it is new, closed-up abbreviations may look "wrong" to those unfamiliar with the rule change. Before closing up the spacing, ask your instructor or supervisor if it is appropriate to use this option.

(c) Beginning Page Number   Rule 3.2(a)

- **Basic Rule:** Provide the page number where the case **begins** in the reporter volume.

(d) Pinpoint Page Number (aka Pincite)   Rules 3.2(a), B10.1.2

- **Basic Rule: All Citations.** Provide the exact page number where the specific material you are citing is located. Separate the beginning page number from the pinpoint page number with a comma and a space.

  Example: Meade v. Sturgill, 467 S.W.2d **363, 365** (Ky. Ct. App. 1971).

☞ To pinpoint in any of the following situations, see Chapter 1 of this guide:

Multiple Pages: To pinpoint material that spans more than one page, or appears on two or more non-consecutive pages, see page 18 of this guide.

First Page: To pinpoint material found on the first page (beginning page) of a case, see page 18 of this guide.

Footnotes: To pinpoint material found in a footnote, see page 22 of this guide.

When to Use a Pinpoint

Pinpoint cites are almost always necessary. The only time a pinpoint is not required is when you are referring to a case in general, without discussing any specific fact, holding, rule, rationale, or other material from the case.

Example of a general statement where pinpoint IS NOT necessary:
   The court addressed liability issues with respect to workers' compensation carriers in <u>Basil v. Wolf</u>, 935 A.2d 1154 (N.J. 2007).

Example of a specific statement where a pinpoint IS necessary:
   The Estate argued that a workers' compensation carrier can be a "third party" capable of being sued directly. <u>Basil v. Wolf</u>, 935 A.2d 1154, 1167 (N.J. 2007).

---

3. Court   Rules 10.4, B10.1.3, Table 1

A full case citation identifies the court that issued the opinion. This section explains how to include court information in your citation and when to omit all or part of the information.

The court information consists of two parts:

(a)   **Jurisdiction:** Identifying the court system that decided the case, either the federal system or a state's system.

(b)   **Court:** Identifying the specific court from that jurisdiction that decided the case. Examples include a circuit court decision from the federal jurisdiction, or a Court of Appeals decision from a state court jurisdiction.

(a)-(b)

| Case Name | + | Volume | + | Reporter Name | + | Beginning Page | + | Pinpoint Page | + | Court | + | Year |

(a)   (b)
Fitzgerald v. Caplan, 362 S.E.2d 103, 105 (**Ga. Ct. App.** 1987).

- **Basic Rule 1.** Identify the (a) jurisdiction and (b) court that decided the case, using the names as they appear in Table 1.1 for federal courts, or Table 1.3 for state courts. Abbreviate exactly as shown in the table, and as discussed in Basic Rule 2, below. Place in parentheses with the year.

- **Basic Rule 2: Abbreviations.** Abbreviate the name of the jurisdiction and court as follows:

   (a)   **Federal Jurisdictions:** For circuit courts, include the abbreviated circuit number followed by the word "Cir." For district courts, include the name of the district court, abbreviated according to Table 1.1 (federal jurisdictions), Table 7 (court names), and Table 10.1 (state names).

Examples:

Tenth Circuit Court of Appeals	☞	10th Cir.
Third Circuit Court of Appeals	☞	3d Cir.
Middle District of Alabama	☞	M.D. Ala.
District of Nevada	☞	D. Nev.

☞ Note that the Second and Third circuits use a two-character abbreviation, **2d** and **3d**, respectively, while all other numbered circuits use a three-character abbreviation: **1st, 4th,** etc.

☞ Do not use superscript for the ordinals: ***Right:*** 8th   ***Wrong:*** 8ᵗʰ

(b) **State Jurisdictions:** The correct abbreviation, if any, is shown immediately after the bold-faced entry for the court in the jurisdiction's Table 1.3 entry.

   ☞ For example, the Table 1.3 entry for Missouri's Court of Appeals looks like this: **Court of Appeals** (Mo. Ct. App.).

   ☞ Do not use the two-letter postal abbreviation to identify a state. Always use the abbreviation shown in Table 1.3 to the right of the court's name.

☞ Be sure to copy the court abbreviation exactly as shown in Table 1, including spacing. Do not rely on abbreviations found in the case itself or in the publisher's own citation for the case—*Bluebook* rules may require a different abbreviation.

✗ **Exception 1: Jurisdiction.** Omit the jurisdiction from the parenthetical if that information is clearly identified by the name of the *reporter*. See examples in the chart on page 39 of this guide.

   ☞ For cases arising in federal courts, the print reporter name identifies the jurisdiction as "federal," either because the reporter name includes the word federal (Federal Reporter, Federal Supplement), or because the reporter only publishes cases from a single federal court.

✗ **Exception 2: Court.** Omit the identity of the court when:

   (a) The court that rendered the decision is that jurisdiction's highest court; or

   (b) The court is clearly identified by the name of the *reporter*.

☞ *Bluebook* Table 1 lists the courts *by rank* under each entry. The highest court always appears first in the table, followed in rank order by the jurisdiction's lower courts.

☞ Omit information identifying a subdivision of the court, such as: (1) division or department names or numbers; (2) the court's location; (3) a state court's district number; or
(4) any smaller subdivision of a federal district court.

Examples:

    (1) Missouri Court of Appeals, Southern District, ~~Division Two~~

    (2) Supreme Court of Tennessee, ~~at Nashville~~

    (3) Illinois Appellate Court, ~~Fifth District~~

    (4) United States District Court, Eastern District of Arkansas, ~~Western Division~~

✗ **Exception:** If the subdivision is particularly relevant to your discussion, it may be included
in the parenthetical. For example, if you are analyzing a split between various districts in
State *X*, it is useful to designate the districts in your citations. See Rule 10.4 and its examples
for guidance on including subdivision information in your citation.

Beware the Coverage Trap

When citing a state (not regional) reporter, check which courts are included in the reporter. Most
states have separate reporters for their highest and intermediate courts of appeals, but occasionally both courts are included in one reporter. Wisconsin Reports and West's California Reporter
are two examples of state reporter sets that publish cases from both their highest and intermediate courts in a single volume. Other jurisdictions may include several lower courts in one set;
for example, the New York Supplement.

When citing a case published in a reporter set that reports more than one court:

☞ All cases: Omit the jurisdiction when it is identified by the name of the reporter.

☞ For cases from the jurisdiction's highest court: In addition to omitting the jurisdiction, omit
the court.

    People v. Powell, 237 Cal. Rptr. 3d 793,798 (2018).

☞ For cases from intermediate or lower courts: Include the court name, as the name of the reporter does not identify the specific court.

    People v. Joseph, 244 Cal. Rptr. 3d 380, 391 (Ct. App. 2019).

Examples: Jurisdiction and Court

Basic Rules 1 & 2	Coburn v. Mayer, 368 S.W.3d 320, 324 (**Mo. Ct. App.** 2012).
Exception 1 *Reporter Name Identifies Jurisdiction but not Court*	Johnson v. Little, 426 **S.C.** 423, 431 (**Ct. App.** 2019). Ljutica v. Holder, 588 **F.3d** 119, 125 (**2d Cir.** 2009). Grote Industries, LLC v. Sebelius, 914 **F. Supp. 2d** 943, 952 (**S.D. Ind.** 2012).
Exception 2 *Highest Court*	People v. Crittenden, 885 P.2d 887, 891 (**Cal.** 1994). Szwed v. State, 89 A.3d 1143, 1147 (**Md.** 2014).
Exceptions 1 & 2 *Reporter Identifies Both Jurisdiction and Court*	Consolver v. Hotze, 51 **Kan. App.** 2d 286, 290 (2015). Holt v. Hobbs, 135 **S. Ct.** 853, 866 (2015).

4. Year   Rules 10.5, B10.1.3

(4)

Case Name	+	Volume	+	Reporter Name	+	Beginning Page	+	Pinpoint Page	+	Court	+	Year

(4)

Fitzgerald v. Caplan, 362 S.E.2d 103, 105 (Ga. Ct. App. **1987**).

- **Basic Rule:** Provide the year the case was **decided**. Omit the month and day.

  ☞ Courts use various terms to identify the date a case was decided. The most common are "decided," "filed," and "issued." Some may just give a date with no further description. No matter what it is called, this is the date to include in the parenthetical.

  ☞ Some opinions also include the date the case was **"argued."** DO NOT include this information in the parenthetical.

  ☞ Some opinions include subsequent history such as "certiorari denied" or "rehearing denied." See discussion of subsequent history on page 65 of this guide.

B. Special Rules for Case Names   Rules 10.2.1, 10.2.2

This section discusses how to treat some common situations that arise with case names.

☞ If you have a situation that does not fit within the categories discussed in this Part, see *Bluebook* Rule 10.1–.2 for guidance.

1. Businesses and Organizations   Rule 10.2.1(a), (c), (h), Tables 6 & 10

- **Basic Rule No. 1: All Citations.** When a business, for-profit or non-profit organization, partnership, or similar entity is a party to the action, include the full name of the entity, including the *form* of the entity, subject to Exceptions 1 and 2, below. Abbreviate terms as described in Basic Rule No. 2, below.

  ☞ Include terms such as Inc., Corp., Co., Ltd., or FSB (a banking term), etc. that follow the entity's name. These terms are part of the party's name.

  ☞ *Do not* include descriptive terms such as "a Delaware corporation" or "a non-profit corporation" that follow the entity's name. For discussion of descriptive terms, see page 47 of this guide.

    Example: Big Business, Incorporated, an Iowa Corporation   ☞   **Big Business, Inc.**

  ☞ Include the given name or initials of a person if that person is part of the company's name.

    Example: **J.K.** Abernathy, Inc. v. **Danny** Pratt Groceries, Ltd.

- ✗ **Exception 1: Double Business Designations.** When a company has **two** of the following (or similar) terms in its name, omit the second term. *Bluebook* R. 10.2.1(h).

Inc.	Ltd.	L.L.C.	N.A.	F.S.B.	R.R.
Ass'n	Bros.	Co.	Corp.	Ins.	

  ☞ *The Bluebook* cautions that dropping the second business designation should be done carefully, and only when the name could not possibly be mistaken for another entity or a natural person.

Examples: Double Business Designation

Name in Caption	Name in Citation	Explanation
Weston Supply **Co., Inc.**	Weston Supply Co.	Both Co. and Inc. appear in R. 10.2.1(h).
Weiss **Insurance Limited**	Weiss Ins.	Both Ins. and Ltd. appear listed in R. 10.2.1(h).

Chart continues on the next page.

Examples: Double Business Designation, *continued*

Name in Caption	Name in Citation	Explanation
Argyle **Brothers Ltd.**	Argyle Bros.	Both Brothers and Ltd. appear in R. 10.2.1(h).
Brothers, Incorporated	Bros. Inc.	Both terms appear in Rule 10.2.1(h), but without Inc., the name could be mistaken for a natural person.

✘ Exception 2: "The" in Case Names. Omit "the" when it **begins** a case name. Retain "the" when it is in the middle of a case name. *Bluebook* R. 10.2.1(d).

Examples:

> **The** Taylor Company v. Jackson   ☞   Taylor Co. v. Jackson
> Benny **the** Clown v. Sharp   ☞   Benny **the** Clown v. Sharp

- **Basic Rule No. 2: Abbreviations in Citation Sentences and Clauses.** Abbreviate the following words appearing in a citation sentence or clause unless it is the only word in the party's name. If the citation is embedded, see Basic Rule No. 5, below.

  (a) Any word appearing in *Bluebook* Table 6 (case name abbreviations), even if it *begins* a party's name.

  (b) Any word appearing in *Bluebook* Table 10 (geographic abbreviations).

  (c) Words of eight or more letters *not* appearing in Table 6, if "substantial" space is saved and the result is "unambiguous in context."

  ☞ In practice, it can be difficult to abbreviate words not found in Table 6 in a way that satisfies both the requirements of saving substantial space and being unambiguous. When in doubt, spell it out.

  Examples:

  > Canada Building Equipment, Incorporated   ☞   Can. Bldg. Equip., Inc.
  > Independent Casualty Society of North America ☞   Indep. Cas. Soc'y of N. Am.

- **Basic Rule No. 3: Plurals.** To form a plural of any word listed in Table 6, add an "s" to the end of the abbreviation. See the introductory paragraph at the top of Table 6 for additional information.

  Examples:

  > Premier Jukebox Authorities   ☞   Premier Jukebox Auths.
  > Chang Publications, Incorporated   ☞   Chang Publ'ns, Inc.

- **Basic Rule No. 4: Widely Known Acronyms.** If the company, organization, or other entity can be identified by an acronym that is well known, use the acronym. DO NOT place periods in the acronym. *Bluebook* R. 6.1(b).

    Examples:

Federal Housing Administration	☞	FHA
National Broadcasting Company	☞	NBC

    ☞ The use of acronyms is optional. If you are not certain if the acronym is "widely known," use the full name.

- **Basic Rule No. 5: Embedded Citations.** In citations embedded in and integral to textual sentences, DO NOT abbreviate the names of parties.

    ✗ **Exception:** Acronyms may be used in embedded citations. In addition, the following eight words are always abbreviated, **UNLESS** the word begins the party's name:

And	☞	&	Corporation	☞	Corp.
Association	☞	Ass'n	Incorporated	☞	Inc.
Brothers	☞	Bros.	Limited	☞	Ltd.
Company	☞	Co.	Number	☞	No.

    Examples:

In a citation sentence:	☞	Can. Bldg. Equip. Inc.
In an embedded citation:	☞	Canada Building Equipment, **Inc.**

2. Governmental Parties (Geographical Terms)   Rule 10.2.1(f)

Many cases involve governmental parties, ranging from the United States and all of its departments, to states, counties, and small towns. *The Bluebook*'s special rules for governmental parties are found in Rule 10.2.1(f), Geographical Terms. Different rules apply to different types of governmental parties. This section discusses the following:

(a) **Federal Government:** If the party is the United States, or any department, division, or agency, see discussion starting on page 43 of this guide.

(b) **State Government:** If the party is a state or commonwealth, the District of Columbia, or a local court in a U.S. territory or possession, including any department, division, or agency, see discussion starting on page 44 of this guide.

(c) **County, City, or Town Government:** If the party is a county or city, including any department, division, agency, or school district, see discussion starting on page 46 of this guide.

Governmental Employees as Parties

Many cases filed against governmental departments or agencies name the director or head as a party. In this situation, it is not necessary to identify the defendant as a governmental employee or include the department or agency in the case name. Apply the rules for individuals to the employee.

For example, "Jane Q. Prisoner" may sue "John Keeper, Warden of the State Penitentiary." In this example, the case name in the citation is: <u>Prisoner v. Keeper</u>.

(a) Federal Government

- **Basic Rule No. 1: United States.** Omit "the" and "of America" from the party's name. Do not abbreviate to "U.S."
- **Basic Rule No. 2: Units, Departments, and Agencies.** Include the full name, including the agency name, abbreviating terms as follows:
  - (1) **In Citation Sentences and Clauses:** Abbreviate any word found in *Bluebook* Tables 6 or 10, including the United States when it is part of a longer name.
  - (2) **In Embedded Citations:** Do not abbreviate any words except the eight words in Rule 10.2.1(c).
- **Basic Rule No. 3: Acronyms.** Well-known acronyms may be used. See discussion of acronyms beginning on page 42 of this guide.
  - ☞ Use acronyms with caution. Be sure that the acronym is truly well known, or that your reader will be familiar with it.

Examples: United States Is a Party

Rule	As It Appears in a Citation Sentence or Clause	As It Appears in an Embedded Citation
Basic Rule No. 1 United States	• <u>United States v. McKinney</u> • <u>Kardem v. United States</u>	• <u>United States v. McKinney</u> • <u>Kardem v. United States</u>
Basic Rule No. 2 Agency or Department	• <u>U.S. Dep't of Agric. v. Binet</u> ☞ See acronym, below • <u>Sayid v. U.S. Border Patrol</u>	• <u>United States Department of Agriculture v. Binet</u> • <u>Sayid v. United States Border Patrol</u>
Basic Rule No. 3 Acronyms	• <u>USDA v. Binet</u>	• <u>USDA v. Binet</u>

(b) State Governments

When a state is a party to the case, how that state is identified depends upon which court issued the opinion. Use the following chart to determine the correct rule to apply.

Chart: When a State Is a Party

If the court issuing the opinion was:	Apply this rule:
A state court	Basic Rule No. 1, below
A federal court	Basic Rule No. 2, below
For simplicity, this table refers to "states." These rules also apply to the District of Columbia, and U.S. territories or jurisdictions listed in Table 1.4.	

- **Basic Rule No. 1: Cases Decided in State Courts.** For cases decided by a court in the *same state*:

    (1) Omit the name of the state, substituting "State," "Commonwealth," or "People," as appropriate. If the name in the case caption includes both "People of" and "State of," use People.

    (2) If the party is a department, agency, or other division of the state government, append the name of the division. In citation sentences and clauses, abbreviate all words according to Tables 6 and 10. In embedded citations, do not abbreviate any words.

Examples: State Is a Party in State Court

Court Issuing Opinion	Name in Caption	Citation *Citation Sentence or Clause*
Georgia	State of Georgia v. Charles	State v. Charles
Kentucky	Commonwealth of Kentucky v. Carlson	Commonwealth v. Carlson
Florida	People of the State of Florida v. Wheeler	People v. Wheeler
Idaho	Idaho Tax Commission v. Jerez	State Tax Comm'n v. Jerez

- **Basic Rule No. 2: Cases Decided in Federal Courts.** For cases decided by a federal court:

    (1) Use the state's name ("Kansas," not "State").

(2) Omit phrases such as "State of" or "People of."

(3) Do not abbreviate if it is the only word in the party's name.

(4) If the party is a department, agency, or other division of the state government, include the name of the division. In citation sentences and clauses, abbreviate all words according to Tables 6 and 10, including the name of the state. In embedded citations, do not abbreviate any words in the agency's name.

Examples: State Is a Party in Federal Court

Court Issuing Opinion	Name in Caption	Citation *Citation Sentence or Clause*
U.S. Supreme	State of Georgia v. Charles	Georgia v. Charles
U.S. 6th Circuit	Commonwealth of Kentucky v. Carlson	Kentucky v. Carlson
U.S. 11th Cir.	People of the State of Florida v. Wheeler	Florida v. Wheeler
U.S. Dist. Ct., Idaho	Idaho Tax Commission v. Jerez	Idaho Tax Comm'n v. Jerez

Notes on Local Practice and State Case Names

Some practitioners prefer to include the name of the state when citing cases from a *different state* than their own.

For example, a practitioner in Connecticut preparing a document to file in a Connecticut court would cite a Connecticut case as **State** v. Dyous, 53 A.3d 153 (Conn. 2012). If, however, the Connecticut practitioner included in the document a citation to a *Vermont* case, the cite according to *Bluebook* rules would be **State** v. Sinclair, 49 A.3d 152 (Vt. 2012). Since both the home state case (Dyous) and the out-of-state Vermont case (Sinclair) are titled "State," the practitioner must rely on the reader noticing that the parenthetical identifies it as an out-of-jurisdiction Vermont case.

Recognizing that a busy reader may overlook the fact that the case is not from the home state of Connecticut—and has a different precedential value—the practitioner may choose to cite the case as **Vermont v. Sinclair** to minimize the chance the case will be mistaken for a Connecticut case.

♦ When citing out-of-jurisdiction cases, ask your instructor or supervisor if the *Bluebook* rule or a local custom should be used in the case name.

(c) A County, City, or Town Is a Party

- **Basic Rule:** Governmental Parties.

  (1) When "County of," "City of," "Town of," or a similar phrase BEGINS the party's name, AND is the entire name of the party, include the phrase in the citation. In addition:

  - Do not include "The" if it precedes the phrase.

  - Do not abbreviate any words if the geographical unit is the *entire name* of the party.

  - Omit geographical designations that follow a comma, such as the name of a state.

    Example: **The City of Chicago v. The County of Cook, Illinois**

    | *Right* | ☞ | City of Chicago v. County of Cook |
    | *Wrong* | ☞ | The City of Chi. v. The Cnty. of Cook, Illinois |

  (2) When the party's name includes **two prepositional phrases**—often a job title followed by the geographic location—omit the second phrase, retaining only the name of the county/city/town.

    Example: **The Sheriff of the County of Broward v. The Mayor of the City of Hollywood, Florida**

    | *Right* | ☞ | Sheriff of Broward v. Mayor of Hollywood |
    | *Wrong* | ☞ | Sheriff of the County of Broward v. Mayor of the City of Hollywood, Florida |

  (3) When a county, city, or town is part of a longer name, include the full name, abbreviating any word found in Table 6 (case names) or table 10.1 (city names).

    Example: **New York City Transit Authority v. New York City Department of Administrative Services**

    | *Right:* | ☞ | N.Y.C. Transit Auth. v. N.Y.C. Dep't of Admin. Servs. |
    | *Wrong* | ☞ | New York City Transit Authority v. New York City Department of Administrative Services |

- **Basic Rule:** Non-Governmental Parties. When a county, city, or town is part of the name of a non-governmental association or private business, include the entity's full name, abbreviating any word found in Table 6 (case names) or table 10.1 (city names).

    Example: **Association of Florists of Baltimore v. Catering Company of Silver Spring**

    | *Right:* | ☞ | Ass'n of Florists of Balt. v. Catering Co. of Silver Spring |
    | *Wrong:* | ☞ | Ass'n of Florists v. Catering Co. of Silver Spring |

3. Alternate Names   Rule 10.2.1(a)

- **Basic Rule:** When a case caption lists alternate names for an individual, business, or other entity, omit the alternate name.

Examples: Alternate Names

Rule 10.2.1(a)	Individuals: Name in Caption	Name in Citation
Also known as	Adele Kite, **a/k/a** Mary Greene	Kite
Formerly known as	Roy A. Watson, **f/k/a** Leroy Watson	Watson
Doing business as	Albert N. Krogh, **d/b/a** Krogh's Cars	Krogh

Rule 10.2.1(a)	Businesses: Name in Caption	Name in Citation
Also known as	Nixon Welding, **a/k/a** Nixon's Auto Welding	Nixon Welding
Formerly known as	J.B. and Associates, **f/k/a** J.B. Company	J.B. & Assocs.
Doing business as	Best Brand Foods, **d/b/a** Brand X	Best Brand Foods

☞ You may encounter other indications of alternate names such as "alias" or "previously known as." No matter the wording, the same rule applies: ignore the alternate name.

4. Procedural and Descriptive Phrases   Rules 10.2.1(b), (e), B10.1.1

Occasionally case names include "procedural" or "descriptive" terms and phrases. Citation rules differ for these two types of phrases, therefore it is important to distinguish them. To sort out these rules, find an example of the term or phrase in the charts below, then consult the Basic Rule indicated.

☞ Procedural phrases precede a party's name.

☞ Procedural phrases describe something about the case as a whole or the type of case or procedural action before the court.

☞ Descriptive phrases follow a party's name.

☞ Descriptive phrases describe something about a party to a case.

Chart 1: Procedural Phrases

If the Caption Says This:	It Is This Type of Procedural Phrase:	Discussed in:
In the Matter of On the Petition of On the Application of In the Matter of the Petition of	Non-adversarial	Basic Rule 1 Page 49
In the Matter of X v. Y On the Petition/Application, etc. of A v. B	Adversarial	Basic Rule 2 Page 49
Ex Parte	Ex Parte	Basic Rule 3 Page 49
On Behalf of For the Use of On the Relation of As next friend of	Relator	Basic Rule 4 Page 49
Estate of Will of Accounting of	Introductory Phrase	Basic Rule 5 Page 50

Chart 2: Descriptive Phrases

If the Caption Says This:	It Is This Type of Descriptive Phrase:	Discussed in:
Trustee for the X Trust Personal Representative of X Estate Administrator of X	Capacity	Basic Rule 6(a) Page 50
Warden, Sheriff, President, Governor, Mayor, Secretary of State, etc. CEO, President, Secretary, etc.	Government office holder/employee Business title	Basic Rule 6(b) Page 50
An Alabama corporation A Federal banking association A not-for-profit partnership	Other	Basic Rule 6(c) Page 50

- **Basic Rule 1: Non-Adversarial.** When there is only one party listed in the caption and the party's name is preceded by one of the procedural phrases identified as "non-adversarial" in Chart 1, shorten the procedural phrase to "In re" and place it before the party's name.

  Examples:

In the Matter of April Hopkins	☞	<u>In re Hopkins</u>
On the Petition of Adan Oluchuku	☞	<u>In re Oluchuku</u>
In the Interests of Henry Veldkamp	☞	<u>In re Veldkamp</u>
In the Matter of the Adoption Petition of J.W.	☞	<u>In re J.W.</u>

- **Basic Rule 2: Adversarial.** When adversarial parties are listed in the caption (e.g., Smith v. Jones) and a party's name is preceded by one of the procedural phrases identified as "Adversarial" in Chart 1, omit the procedural phrase.

  Examples:

In the Matter of Jason Davis v. Sam Tribe	☞	<u>Davis v. Tribe</u>
On the Petition of Mark Wilson v. Ann Clark	☞	<u>Wilson v. Clark</u>

- **Basic Rule 3: Ex Parte.** When there is only *one party* listed in the caption and the party's name is preceded by the words "ex parte," include the procedural phrase "Ex parte," placing it before the party's name.

  ☞ The phrase "ex parte" is used when only one party in an adversarial action is seeking relief from the court. That party is said to be appearing before the court "ex parte." Often the full name of the case appears in parentheses in the caption; omit the parenthetical case name from the citation.

  Examples:

Ex parte Gail Cannon	☞	<u>Ex parte Cannon</u>
Ex parte Karla Vega (Karla Vega v. Mark Vega)	☞	<u>Ex parte Vega</u>

- **Basic Rule 4: Relator.** When the procedural phrase precedes a party's name indicating a person is acting on behalf of another party, shorten the procedural phrase to "ex rel." Include the name of the representative (the relator) followed by "ex rel.," then the name of the represented party.

  ☞ Relators are persons or entities who institute or defend proceedings on behalf of another party. These cases often involve parents, guardians, or the state, taking action on behalf of minor children or legally incompetent persons. The represented party is often identified by initials to protect privacy.

  ✗ Exception: When a relator (representative) sues individually **and** on behalf of someone else, include only the relator's name. In other words, the ordinary multiple-party rules apply. See the last example, below.

Examples: Relators

Carefully read the caption to determine which party is the relator and which party is represented. Place the relator's name first in the citation, followed by "ex rel." then the represented person's name. This may require you to name the parties in a different order than they appear in the caption, as shown in the first example below.

Caption	Relator	Citation
Juan Flores, **by and through his Sister and Next Friend**, Carmen Diaz v. Mercy Medical Center	Diaz	Diaz ex rel. Flores v. Mercy Med. Ctr.
Leonard Woods **on behalf of** Chris Woods, a minor v. Allen Ellis	Woods	Woods ex. rel. Woods v. Ellis
K.C.R. v. State of Utah, **in the interest of** C.R., F.R., A.R., and W.R.	State	K.C.R. v. State ex rel. C.R.
The State of Washington **on the Relation of** Vincent Gibson v. Harrison Glenn	State	State ex rel. Gibson v. Glenn
✗ Eric Lynch, **individually, and on behalf of** his minor daughter Sarah Lynch v. Jane E. Kennedy	Eric Lynch	Lynch v. Kennedy ☞Multi-party rule applies

- **Basic Rule 5: Introductory Phrases.** When a party's name is preceded by an introductory phrase, include the phrase in both adversarial and non-adversarial cases.

  ♦ Underline or italicize both the introductory phrase and case name.

    Examples:

Will of Dominic Strickland	☞	Will of Strickland
Estate of Bridget Blair v. Tower Insurance	☞	Estate of Blair v. Tower Ins.
Jerry Josephs v. Estate of Karen Zur	☞	Josephs v. Estate of Zur

- **Basic Rule 6: Descriptive Phrases.** Omit all terms or phrases following a party's name that describe:

  (a) The party's capacity as a representative of someone else, such as administrator, executor, trustee, etc.;

  (b) The person's governmental or professional position, or other job title; and

  (c) All terms describing a business party or other entity such as "a Nebraska corporation" or "a not-for-profit corporation."

Examples: Descriptive Phrases

Type of Phrase	Phrase in Caption	Citation
Capacity	Mike Beyer, **Trustee for the Wilson Trust** v. Jessie Parks, **Administer of the Leigh Estate**	Beyer v. Parks
	Q. A. Nader, **Personal Representative of the Estate of** Sabihah Samaha v. Lydia Mejia	Nader v. Mejia
Job and Professional Titles	Eric Crane **Esq.** v. **Dr.** Salvatore Eddy, **M.D.**	Crane v. Eddy
	Ed Kohl, **CEO/President** of Ace, Inc. v. Peter Roundson, **Secretary of State**	Kohl v. Roundson
	Ann Carter, **Warden** v. Megan Rivers, **Mayor**	Carter v. Rivers
Other	Shark Industries, **an Alabama Corp.** v. Baxter Center, a **non-profit corporation**	Shark Indus. v. Baxter Ctr.

5. Unions   Rule 10.2.1(i)

Union names are often long and complicated. Always consult *Bluebook* Rule 10.2.1(i) when a union is a party, and follow the examples closely.

- **Basic Rule:** Include the "smallest unit" that accurately describes the union. If the union is widely known by an acronym, use the acronym initials, following *Bluebook* Rule 10.2.1(c). In addition:

  (a) Include the name and number of the **local** union, if any.

  (b) Omit any words or phrases of location such as a city, state, or region.

  (c) If the union represents several different industries or crafts, include only the industry or craft listed first.

  (d) In citation sentences and clauses, abbreviate any words appearing in Tables 6 or 10. In embedded citations, do not abbreviate any words except the eight words in Rule 10.2.1(c).

  Examples:

Caption:	Sheet Metal Workers' International, Local Union 15 of Northern California, AFL-CIO
Citation Sentence:	Sheet Metal Workers Int'l, Loc. 15
Embedded Citation:	Sheet Metal Workers International, Local 15

6. Commissioner of Internal Revenue   Rule 10.2.1(j)

- **Basic Rule:** Shorten the name to "Commissioner." In citation sentences and clauses, abbreviate to "Comm'r"; do not abbreviate in embedded citations.

  Examples:

Caption:	Commissioner of Internal Revenue v. Bruno Matthews
Citation Sentence:	<u>Comm'r v. Matthews</u>
Embedded Citation:	<u>Commissioner v. Matthews</u>

C. Short Form Case Citations   Rules 4.1, 10.9, B10.2

Once a case has been cited in full, subsequent references to that case may be shortened. The two short forms that can be used for case citations are discussed in detail below. Also see the discussion of general rules for short form citations starting on page 26 of this guide. This Part discusses the following:

1. <u>Id.</u>, when citing the same case as the immediately preceding citation;

2. Alternate short form, for use after an intervening citation to different authority.

☞ Adaptations that may be necessary when using parallel citations and public domain formats are discussed in their respective sections of this guide.

1. <u>Id.</u>   Rules 4.1, 10.9, B10.2

<u>Id.</u> is used to cite the **same** authority as was cited in the **immediately preceding citation**. It may be used with or without a new pinpoint. See discussion of the general rules for <u>id.</u> short form citations on page 26 of this guide. Use <u>id.</u> only in citation sentences and clauses, never in embedded citations.

- **Basic Rule No. 1: Same Page.** When pinpointing the **same page** of the **same case**, include <u>id.</u> by itself; no page number is necessary. ♦ Underline or italicize <u>id.</u>, including the period. Capitalize <u>id.</u> when it begins a citation sentence, but use lowercase in a citation clause.

- **Basic Rule No. 2: Different Page.** When pinpointing a different page of the same case, include <u>id.</u> followed by "at" and the new pinpoint page number.

☞ Special rules apply when the preceding citation contains more than one authority. See discussion of string citations in Chapter 9, Part A of this guide.

Examples:

| Same Page | ☞ | <u>Id.</u> | *or* | <u>id.</u> |
| Different Page | ☞ | <u>Id.</u> at 213 | *or* | <u>id.</u> at 213. |

Caution: <u>Id.</u> Is a Citation, Not a Substitute Case Name

Wrong: As a result, the court concluded in **<u>id.</u>** at 474 that the trial court properly rendered summary judgment in favor of the co-defendant.

Right: As a result, the court concluded in **<u>Sherman</u>** that the trial court properly rendered summary judgment in favor of the co-defendant. **<u>Id.</u>** at 474.

---

2. Alternate Short Form   **Rules 10.9, B10.2**

When <u>id.</u> cannot be used because of one or more intervening citations to different authority, use the following **alternate short form.**

- **Basic Rule No. 1: Alternate Form.** Provide ONLY the information listed below, in ordinary type. Omit all other information typically found in a full citation, including the beginning page number, court information, and year.

  (1) Name of the case, shortened as described in Basic Rules 2 and 3, below, ♦ underlined or italicized;

  (2) Volume number;

  (3) Reporter name, abbreviated according to *Bluebook* Table 1;

  (4) The word "at"; and

  (5) A pinpoint page number, whether it is a new page number or the same page as the prior citation to the same case.

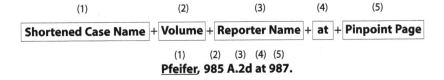

	(1)		(2)		(3)		(4)		(5)
	Shortened Case Name	+	Volume	+	Reporter Name	+	at	+	Pinpoint Page

(1) (2) (3) (4) (5)
<u>Pfeifer</u>, 985 A.2d at 987.

- **Basic Rule No. 2: Case Name.** To identify the case in the short form, use the **first party** listed in the full citation; omit the other party.

    ✗ **Exception 1: Common Litigants.** If the first party listed in the full citation is a common or frequent litigant choose the *second* party for your shortened case name.

    ☞ Many governmental units, agencies, or officials engage in frequent litigation. For example, states are parties to thousands of criminal cases each year, as is the United States government. If you are writing a brief in a state criminal matter, you may cite dozens of cases that are all named "State v. X." In the alternate short form, all those cases would be shortened to "State," making it impossible to distinguish one case from another. To avoid confusion, use the second party's name.

    ☞ A couple of other well-known common litigants are the ACLU and NAACP.

    ☞ Businesses are not considered common litigants, even though some are frequently involved in litigation (e.g., large insurance companies).

    ✗ **Exception 2: Two Cases with Same Name.** If your document will include short form citations to two cases with the same name (e.g., two cases where the first party is State Farm Ins., or two parties with the surname Miller), choose the *second party* for one or both of the cases to avoid confusion.

- **Basic Rule No. 3: Shortening Long Names.** You may shorten longer names of businesses or organizations following these guidelines:

    (a) Retain enough of the name so that it cannot be confused with a person's last name. Generally two words is sufficient.

    (b) Do not shorten to one word unless the party is very well known and it cannot be confused with an individual. Examples include Walmart and Exxon.

    (c) Drop Inc., Co., Corp. and similar terms **unless** it would leave only a single word.

    Examples:

Full Citation:	☞	Wilmington Savings Society, FSB
Alternate Short Form:	☞	Wilmington Savings
But not:	☞	Wilmington
		(possible confusion with person's last name)

- **Basic Rule No. 4: Procedural Phrases.** When the full citation contains a procedural phrase, retain that phrase in the short form.

    Examples:

Full Citation:	☞	In re Veldkamp
Alternate Short Form:	☞	In re Veldkamp

- **Basic Rule No. 5: Split Citations.** A split citation is one where the case name appears in the text sentence but the rest of the citation appears in a citation sentence following the text. Although *The Bluebook* does not authorize split citations when a case is cited in full, they may be used with short forms to avoid repeating the case name in short succession.

☞ For further discussion of split citations, see page 16 of this guide.

Examples:

Optional Split Citation: Since both prongs of the standard were satisfied in **Byers**, the court held they were entitled to conduct-based implied antitrust immunity. **600 F.3d at 295.**

Without Split Citation: Since both prongs of the standard were satisfied in **Byers**, the court held they were entitled to conduct-based implied antitrust immunity. **Byers, 600 F.3d at 295.**

More About Split Citations

Use split citations with caution. If there is any chance your reader might be confused as to which case you are discussing, include the case name with the citation that follows the text.

In theory, an alternate short form citation can be used *without* the name appearing in either the text sentence or in the citation sentence at the end. Revising the previous example from the Byers decision, the sentence and citation would read:

Since both prongs of the standard were satisfied, the court held they were entitled to conduct-based implied antitrust immunity. **600 F.3d at 295.**

Keep in mind, however, lawyers remember cases by name, not source information. To determine which case is cited, your reader will be forced to backtrack. Since this is an alternate short form, the last case cited was not the Byers case, but a different authority. Although you *can* use this type of short form—without the case name—that doesn't mean you *should*.

Examples: Alternate Short Forms

	Case Name in Full Citation	Case Name in Short Form
Basic Alternate Short Form	**Purtell v. Mason**, 527 F.3d 615, 621 (7th Cir. 2008). **Ricci v. DeStefano**, 557 U.S. 557, 577 (2009).	**Purtell**, 527 F.3d at 622. **Ricci**, 557 U.S. at 578.
Common Litigant	**State v. Montgomery**, 39 So. 3d 252, 256 (Fla. 2010). **United States v. Vizcarra**, 668 F.3d 516, 522 (7th Cir. 2012).	**Montgomery**, 39 So. 3d at 257. **Vizcarra**, 668 F.3d at 522.
Shortened Name	**Baptist Mem'l Hosp.** v. Sebelius, 768 F. Supp. 2d 295, 300 (D.D.C. 2011).	**Baptist Mem'l**, 768 F. Supp. 2d at 301.
	Wal-Mart Stores, Inc. v. Crossgrove, 276 P.3d 562, 568 (Colo. 2012).	**Wal-Mart**, 276 P.3d at 568. ☞ *Well-known name.*
	Superior Oil Co. v. Fulmer, 785 F.2d 252, 258 (8th Cir. 1986). **Pas, Inc.** v. Engel, 350 S.W.3d 602, 609 (Tex. Ct. App. 2011).	**Superior Oil**, 785 F.2d at 259. **Pas, Inc.**, 350 S.W.3d at 610. ☞ *Dropping "Inc." leaves only one word in name.*
Procedural Phrase	**In re Jackson**, 51 A.3d 529, 537 (D.C. 2012). **Estate of Stephens** v. Galen Health Care, 911 So. 2d 277, 282 (Fla. Dist. Ct. App. 2005).	**In re Jackson**, 51 A.3d at 536. **Estate of Stephens**, 911 So. 2d at 279.
Split Citation	**State v. Jordan**, 33 A.3d 307, 315 (Conn. App. Ct. 2012).	As stated in **Jordan**, prosecutorial impropriety claims invoke a two step analysis. **33 A.3d at 315.**

Example: Short Forms In Context

A patient cannot sue for intentional infliction of emotional distress based on "negligent misinformation." [1] **Fitzgerald v. Caplan, 362 S.E.2d 103, 105 (Ga. Ct. App. 1987).** In Fitzgerald, a doctor wrote a cancer diagnosis on a patient's insurance claim form intending to "fit the plaintiff's insurance claim into one of the pre-ordained diagnostic categories considered compensable by her insurance carrier." [2] **Id. at 104.** The court found that although the physician inserted the words "Determine Extent of Malignancy" in the space designated "Diagnosis of nature of illness or injury," [3] **id.,** the doctor's act did not fall into the category of misconduct acts which are of an "outrageous or egregious nature," [4] **id. at 105.**

In applying the rule, the court reviewed and then declined to follow [5] **Stafford v. Neurological Medical, Inc., 811 F.2d 470 (8th Cir. 1987),** where the doctor's misconduct was virtually identical but the nature of the claims was different, [6] **Fitzgerald, 362 S.E.2d at105.** In **Stafford,** the plaintiff stated an additional claim based upon negligence and recovered on that basis. [7] **811 F.2d at 475. Fitzgerald** was founded solely on a claim of intentional infliction of emotional distress. [8] **362 S.E.2d at 105.** The court concluded in Fitzgerald that claiming intentional infliction of emotional distress based on mere "negligent information" is a contradiction in terms. [9] **Id.**

[1] First mention of Fitzgerald: Full citation used.

[2] Fitzgerald cited again, no intervening citation: Id. used with new pinpoint.

[3] Fitzgerald cited again, no intervening citation, same page, citation clause: id. used without pinpoint.

[4] Fitzgerald cited again, no intervening citation, different page, citation clause: id. used with new pinpoint.

[5] First mention of Stafford; citation clause: Full citation.

[6] Fitzgerald cited again after intervening citation to Stafford; citation clause: Alternate short form used.

[7] Stafford cited after intervening citation to Fitzgerald: Alternate short form with split citation.

[8] Fitzgerald cited after intervening citation to Stafford: Alternate short form with split citation.

[9] Fitzgerald cited again, no intervening citation, same page: Id. used without pinpoint.

D. Parallel Citations   Rules 10.3.1, B10.1.3

Many court opinions are published in multiple print reporters, and case captions frequently include citations to two, three, or even more reporters. These are known as **parallel citations**.

The Bluebook **requires citation to one source only.** However, local rules in some states require citation to that state's official reporter AND to the regional reporter. As a practitioner, you must conform to local rules.

♦ While learning legal citation, your instructor may ask you to conform to *Bluebook* rules, citing just one source. Be sure to ask if parallel citations are required.

Fitzgerald v. Caplan, **184 Ga. App. 567, 568, 362 S.E.2d 103, 105** (Ga. Ct. App. 1987).

• **Basic Rule No. 1: All Parallel Citations.** When parallel citations are required, provide the source information for each reporter cited, with pinpoint pages for *all* sources. Separate the parallel citations with a *comma*. Follow the rules for source information discussed in Part A of this chapter.

    ☞ If one or more of the reporters identifies the jurisdiction or court, omit that information from the parenthetical.

    Examples:

    Marengo Cave Co. v. Ross, **212 Ind. 624, 630, 10 N.E.2d 917, 920** (1937).

    Dunn v. Blumstein, **405 U.S. 330, 343, 92 S. Ct. 995, 1002, 31 L. Ed. 2d 274, 285** (1972).

• **Basic Rule No. 2: Short Form.** Follow the rules for case short forms described in Part C of this chapter, with the following modifications. See examples in the chart, below.

    (1) **Modified Id.:** After id., include the following:

        (a) For the first source, include the word "at" followed by pinpoint. Include the pinpoint information even if citing to the same page.

        (b) For the second and each additional source, include the volume, reporter, "at" and pinpoint. Separate each source with a comma. To cite a different page of the first source, follow id. with "at" and the new pinpoint.

Examples:

Same page:	Id. at 27, 352 N.W.2d at 519.
Different page:	Id. at 29, 352 N.W.2d at 522.
Three Sources:	Id. at 123, 105 S. Ct. at 2528, 86 L. Ed. 2d at 89.

(2) **Modified Alternate Short Form.** Include the case name followed by the source information (volume, reporter, pinpoint) for *all* sources, separated by commas.

Examples:

Ming Yu He, 207 N.J. at 233, 24 A.3d at 259.

Philip Morris, 549 U.S. at 350, 127 S. Ct. at 1061, 166 L. Ed. 2d at 944.

E. Public Domain Citations   Rule 10.3.3

About fifteen jurisdictions have adopted a public domain citation format for documents submitted to their courts. Also known as "medium neutral" or "universal" citations, these forms do not refer to or rely on a particular publisher, and do not have reporter names or volume numbers. Pinpoints in public domain citations may be either to paragraphs or pages, with pages always starting at 1.

If a state has adopted a public domain format, it appears at the top of the state's entry in Table 1.3, together with the effective date and examples of the state's form. Although state public domain forms vary, they *usually* include the following information, although not necessarily in this order:

(1) Case name;

(2) Year of decision;

(3) Jurisdiction, usually in the form of the state's two-character postal code;

(4) Deciding court, abbreviated as shown in the public domain form in Table 1.3, unless the case is from the jurisdiction's highest court;

(5) Decision or docket number: the sequential number of the decision (found in the court caption);

(6) Pinpoint paragraph number, using the paragraph symbol [¶], or page number, with or without a "p." for page number; and

(7) Parallel citation(s) to the regional reporter.

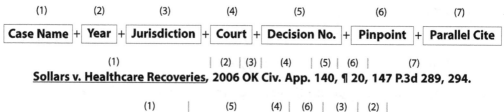

(1)	(2)	(3)	(4)	(5)	(6)	(7)
Case Name	+ Year	+ Jurisdiction	+ Court	+ Decision No.	+ Pinpoint	+ Parallel Cite

(1) | (2) | (3) | (4) | (5) | (6) | (7)
Sollars v. Healthcare Recoveries, 2006 OK Civ. App. 140, ¶ 20, 147 P.3d 289, 294.

(1) | (5)   (4) | (6) | (3) | (2) |
Brown v. Tate, 11-CA-00335-COA (¶ 16) (Miss. 2011).

☞ The public domain entry in Table 1.3 shows at least two examples of public domain citations for each jurisdiction. The first (usually) shows a citation *without* a pinpoint, while the second shows the same citation *with* a pinpoint. Or the two forms may differ in other ways. It might take a little detective work to find the differences between the examples.

- **Basic Rule No. 1: All Citations.** Use the state's required format for all cases after the **effective date.** For cases decided before the effective date, use standard *Bluebook* form.

  ☞ The effective date is found under the state's Table 1.3 listing. Look for language similar to this: [State] has adopted a public domain citation format for cases after [date].

- **Basic Rule No. 2: Pinpoints.** To pinpoint, follow the jurisdiction's example in Table 1.3, pinpointing either paragraphs or pages as indicated in the Table.

  (a) **Paragraphs:** When the state divides cases into paragraphs, individual paragraphs are numbered and marked with a paragraph symbol.

  (b) **Pages:** When the state divides cases into pages, the page numbers are usually indicated in the citation with an asterisk (star), or a lower case "p." for page

- **Basic Rule No. 3: Parallel Citations.** Most jurisdictions require parallel citations to a regional or state reporter (or both). See discussion of parallel citations in Part D of this chapter.

  ☞ Although a state's form may not require pinpoints to the regional reporter, it is courteous to include pinpoints in your citation.

- **Basic Rule No. 4: Unpublished Decisions.** If the decision is unpublished, add a "U" after the decision number. Omit a parallel citation (as none is available).

  Example: Flippen v. Jones, 2014 Ark. App. **220U,** at 2.

- **Basic Rule No. 5: Short Forms.** *The Bluebook* does not provide a specific short form for public domain citations. Applying the ordinary rules for short forms for cases discussed in Part C of this chapter, adapt short forms as follows:

  (a) **Id.:** Use id. with the pinpoint paragraph or page number. Include "at" between id. and the pinpoint only when citing **pages.** When using the **paragraph symbol**, do not use "at." Follow with the modified short form for the parallel citation. See discussion of parallel citation short forms in Part D of this chapter.

(b) **Alternate Short Form:** When id. cannot be used, a modified short form that includes the case name, followed by the decision number, the word "at," the pinpoint paragraph or page number, then a modified citation for all parallel citations. See discussion of parallel citation short forms in Part D of this chapter.

Example 1: Public Domain Citations to Paragraphs

Gregory Coyne v. Greg Peace SUPREME JUDICIAL COURT OF MAINE 2004 ME 150; 863 A.2d 885 December 14, 2004, Decided	
Full citation to paragraphs	<u>Coyne v. Peace</u>, 2004 ME 150, ¶8, 863 A.2d 885, 889.
Id. with same paragraph and same page	<u>Id.</u>
Id. with different paragraph and different page	<u>Id.</u> ¶**12**, 863 A.2d at **890**.
Id. with same paragraph and different page	<u>Id.</u> ¶**12**, 863 A.2d at **891**.
Alternate Short Form	<u>Coyne</u>, 2004 ME 150, ¶8, 863 A.2d at 889.

Example 2: Public Domain Citations to Pages

Mary P. Ogea v. Travis Merritt and Merritt Construction, LLC. SUPREME COURT OF LOUISIANA No. 2013-C-1085 130 So. 3d 888 December 10, 2013	
Full citation to pages	<u>Ogea v. Merritt</u>, 13-C-1085, p. 6, (La. 12/10/13), 130 So. 3d 888, 895.
Id. with same page	<u>Id.</u>
Id. with different pages	<u>Id.</u> at **p. 11**, 29 So. 3d at **897**.
Id. with same page in first source and different page in second source	<u>Id.</u> at **p. 11**, 29 So. 3d at **896–97**.
Alternate Short Form	<u>Ogea</u>, 2013-C-1085, p. 7, 130 So. 3d at 895.

F. Parenthetical Information   Rules 10.6, B10.1.5

Sometimes additional details about the precedential value of a cited decision may be necessary or useful. This information is appended to the end of the citation in a separate parenthetical. This section discusses the following common situations:

1. Citing dissents and concurrences, beginning on this page;

2. Using quoting and citing parentheticals, beginning on page 63; and

3. Indicating the "weight of authority" for decisions rendered en banc, per curiam, etc., beginning on page 64.

☞ The parentheticals discussed in this section are distinct from "explanatory parentheticals." Explanatory parentheticals provide details about the facts, holding, rationale, or other information about a case. Explanatory parentheticals are discussed in Chapter 9, beginning on page 131.

1. Dissents and Concurrences   Rule 10.6.1

When citing material from a dissenting or concurring opinion, **always** indicate that information in a parenthetical at the end of the citation. Failing to note this misleads the court about the weight of the cited material and may result in a court issuing sanctions against the offending lawyer. Don't do it!

- **Basic Rule:** In a separate parenthetical placed immediately after the date parenthetical, include the judge's surname, followed by a "J." (for judge or justice), a comma, and the words "dissenting" or "concurring," as appropriate.

  ☞ Include a space between the date parenthetical and the dissenting/concurring parenthetical.

Examples: Dissents and Concurrences

Dissent	The dissent noted that the same conditions did not exist, therefore a similar level of force could not be supported on the facts. <u>Cotton v. State</u>, 872 A.2d 87, 102 (Md. 2005) (**Battaglia, J., dissenting**).
Concurrence	The district court sees and hears the witnesses, and it is not up to the appellate court to decide whether the witnesses were telling the truth. <u>Beaver v. Mont. Dep't of Nat. Res. & Conservation</u>, 78 P.3d 857, 876 (Mont. 2003) (**Warner, J., concurring**).

2. Quoting or Citing Parentheticals   Rule 10.6.3

The precedent-based U.S. legal system means opinions frequently quote from or cite to prior opinions or other authority. Sometimes you may want to indicate to your reader that the case you used to support your proposition was itself relying on earlier authority.

- To indicate that you are quoting material from a case that in turn was quoting from another authority, use a **"quoting parenthetical."**

- To indicate that you are quoting or paraphrasing material from a case that in turn relied on (but did not quote) another authority, use a **"citing parenthetical."**

- **Basic Rule No. 1: Quoting Parentheticals.** Use a quoting parenthetical when quoting material from one case that in turn was quoting from another authority. In a separate parenthetical placed immediately after the date parenthetical, include the word "quoting" followed by a full citation, with pinpoint, to the original source. Include a space between the date and quoting parentheticals.

  ☞ Look closely at the examples below and the note at the bottom of the chart about using two closing parentheses.

- **Basic Rule No. 2: Citing Parentheticals.** Use a citing parenthetical when citing material from one case that in turn cites another authority. In a separate parenthetical placed immediately after the date parenthetical, include the word "citing" followed by a full citation, with pinpoint, to the original source. Include a space between the date and citing parentheticals.

  ☞ Frequently courts do not use *Bluebook* citation form when citing to prior decisions. Always place citations to prior cases in *Bluebook* form in your document, even if the court did not.

- **Basic Rule No. 3: Level of Recursion.** If the cited material is derived from a chain of prior cases—referred to as levels of recursion—cite only the first level, i.e., the first prior authority.

  ☞ For example, if you are citing to Case No. 1, which quotes from Case No. 2, which cites to Case No. 3, etc., stop after Case 2.

  ☞ *The Bluebook* allows additional levels of recursion if the "information conveyed is particularly relevant." For practitioners, this would rarely, if ever, be required. If the prior cases are particularly relevant, those cases should be discussed in the text and cited directly.

Examples: Quoting and Citing Parentheticals

Quoting Parenthetical	"A court properly exercises its discretion if it examines relevant facts, applies a proper standard of law and, using a demonstrated rational process, reaches a conclusion that a reasonable judge could reach." Smith v. Golde, 592 N.W.2d 287, 291 (Wis. Ct. App. 1999) (**quoting** Kerans v. Manion Outdoors Co., 482 N.W.2d 110, 113 (Wis. Ct. App. 1992)).

Chart continues on the next page.

Examples: Quoting and Citing Parentheticals, *continued*

Citing Parenthetical	A defendant must "purposefully avail" itself of the privilege of conducting business activities within Texas to invoke the benefits and protections of Texas laws. <u>Am. Type Culture Collection, Inc. v. Coleman</u>, 83 S.W.3d 801, 806 (Tex. 2002) (**citing** <u>Burger King Corp. v. Rudzewicz</u>, 471 U.S. 462, 475 (1985)).
Levels of Recursion	"No one is entitled to judicial relief for a supposed or threatened injury until the prescribed administrative remedy has been exhausted." <u>Woodford v. Ngo</u>, 548 U.S. 81, 110 (2006) (**quoting** <u>McKart v. United States</u>, 395 U.S. 185, 193 (1969)) (~~citing Myers v. Bethlehem Shipbuilding Corp., 303 U.S. 41, 50–51 (1938)~~).

> ☞ **Notice the "extra" closing parenthesis at the end of quoting or citing parentheticals. When a parenthetical is nested inside another parenthetical, each must have a closing parenthesis. Here, the date parentheticals nest inside the quoting or citing parentheticals, requiring two closing parentheses.**

3. Weight of Authority   Rules 10.6.1, B10.1.5

A parenthetical statement can be added to the end of a citation to provide additional information about the relative "weight" or precedential value of a case. For example, to indicate that the entire court rendered the decision, not just a three-judge panel, include the word en banc in a parenthetical. Other common weight-of-authority parentheticals include per curiam (indicating the opinion was authored by the court as a whole instead of a single judge); or 5–4 decision (indicating the court was closely divided on the question).

- **Basic Rule:** Include the appropriate information indicating the weight of the authority in a separate parenthetical placed immediately following the date parenthetical.

☞ Include a space between the date parenthetical and the weight of authority parenthetical.

☞ It is not necessary to italicize foreign words or phrases in a weight of authority parenthetical as the usual terms have passed into common English usage. For additional information, see *Bluebook* Rule 7.

Examples: Weight of Authority

En Banc	<u>Waters v. Thomas</u>, 46 F.3d 1506, 1512 (11th Cir. 1995) **(en banc)**.
Plurality	<u>Troxel v. Granville</u>, 530 U.S. 57, 69 (2000) **(plurality opinion)**.
5–4 Decision	<u>Laster v. State</u>, 275 S.W.3d 512, 521 (Tex. Crim. App. 2009) **(5–4 decision)**.
Per Curiam	<u>Collier v. Barnhart</u>, 473 F.3d 444, 448 (2d Cir. 2007) **(per curiam)**.

G. Subsequent History   Rules 10.7, B10.1.6

Once an opinion is issued by a court, the case is not necessarily over. A party may appeal to a higher court, the case may be remanded to the trial court for retrial, etc. The following explains how to include subsequent history in full citations.

- **Basic Rule:** Provide the subsequent history after the date parenthetical if the case was addressed by the *same or higher court*, separated from the main citation by a comma. Do not place in parentheses. In addition:

  a. Begin with the appropriate word or phrase (e.g., reversed, affirmed, overruled, etc.), ♦ underlined or italicized, and abbreviated as shown in *Bluebook* Table 8.

  b. Follow with a citation to the subsequent case that includes: (1) source information, without a pinpoint; (2) jurisdiction and court of subsequent decision; and (3) date of subsequent decision, **unless** it is the same year as the main case. Only include the case name if it is different from the main case.

✗ Exception: Unless it is relevant to the point you are making, omit the following:

- Denials of certiorari **more than two years old;**

- The history on remand if the case was remanded to a lower court for further proceedings; and

- Denials of rehearing.

Examples: Subsequent History

Reversed by a higher court	People v. Hawthorne, 692 N.W.2d 879, 884 (Mich. Ct. App. 2005), rev'd, 713 N.W.2d 724 (Mich. 2006).
Affirmed by a higher court	State v. Thompson, 34 P.3d 382, 386–87 (Ariz. Ct. App. 2001), aff'd, 65 P.3d 420 (Ariz. 2003).
Affirmed by *same* court, *same* year	Baker v. Commonwealth, 486 S.E.2d 111, 114 (Va. Ct. App. 1997), aff'd en banc, 493 S.E.2d 687.
New name on subsequent decision	State v. Murdock, 323 P.3d 846, 852 (2014), overruled by State v. Keel, 357 P.3d 251 (2015).
Certiorari denied	Davis v. Kent, 444 P.3d 456, 466 (N.M. 2019), cert. denied, 140 S. Ct. 884 (2020).

H. Ordering Multiple Additions to Citations   Rules 10.6.4, 1.5(b)

When a citation has more than one type of parenthetical information or subsequent history appended, that appended information must be placed in a specific order as provided in *Bluebook* Rule 1.5

- **Basic Rule:** Prepare the parenthetical(s) or subsequent history following *Bluebook* rules and the discussion for each type of information found in this guide. Once prepared, place the the information in the order listed below. Do not use punctuation between parentheticals, but leave a space. If the citation includes subsequent history—which is not placed in parentheses—separate the subsequent history with a comma.

  1. Weight of authority (en banc);

  2. Dissents or concurrence;

  3. Weight of authority (plurality opinion, per curiam);

  4. Quoting or citing parentheticals;

  5. Explanatory parentheticals; and

  6. Subsequent history.

☞ If you encounter more complex situations than shown in this guide, see *Bluebook* Rule 1.5(b).

Examples: Order of Multiple Additions Appended to Citations

Additional Appended Information	Example
[1] Weight **[6] Subsequent history**	Spears v. United States, 469 F.3d 1166 (2006) [1] **(en banc),** [6] **vacated** 552 U.S. 1090 (2008).
[5] Explanatory parenthetical **[6] Subsequent history**	Naevus Int'l, Inc. v. AT&T Corp., 713 N.Y.S.2d 642 (Sup. Ct. 2000) [5] **(breach of contract claim** was about the quality of service), [6] **modified,** 724 N.Y.S.2d 721 (Sup. Ct. 2001).
[2] Dissent **[3] Weight (per curiam)** **[5] Explanatory parenthetical** **[6] Subsequent history**	United States v. Seale, 570 F.3d 650, 651 (5th Cir. 2009) [2] (DeMoss, J., **dissenting)** [3] **(per curiam)** [5] **(noting** the "nominal" nature in light of the deadlock), [6] **aff'd,** 130 S. Ct. 12 (2010).

3 Statutes

Bluebook Whitepages Rule 12 and Bluepages Rule B12 control the form for statutory citations.

The legislative branches of the federal government and each state enact laws governing the affairs within their borders. The body of law for a jurisdiction is referred to as its "code," and is published in multi-volume sets called "code sets." Individual laws found within the code are called "statutes" or "code sections."

Jurisdictions differ on how they organize statutes within their code sets. All jurisdictions use some type of grouping to keep statutes on a particular topic together. Most use a combination of titles, articles, and chapters, but there are variations. Some jurisdictions include these subdivisions in their citation forms, while others do not. *Bluebook* Table 1 will show you what to include in your citation

☞ Statutes are available in print sources, online from the jurisdiction itself, and from commercial databases such as Westlaw, LEXIS, and Fastcase. This chapter discusses print sources only. To cite statutes from commercial databases, see Chapter 13 of this guide.

This chapter addresses the following:

A. Basic federal and state statutory citations, beginning on the next page;

B. Additional information that may be required including citing to supplements, subject matter codes, and named statutes, beginning on page 76; and

C. Short form citations, beginning on page 77.

Before embarking on statutory citations, it is helpful to keep a few things in mind:

☞ **Typefaces:** By tradition, practitioners use ordinary type for all parts of statutory citations, while academics use LARGE AND SMALL CAPITALS. The rules have recently changed. Before using LARGE AND SMALL CAPITALS, see discussion of typefaces in Chapter 1, beginning on page 6.

☞ **Dates:** The examples shown throughout this chapter are actual authorities in force at the time of publication. Code sets are continuously updated as statutes are enacted, revised, or repealed. Each jurisdiction follows its own publication schedule for printing code sets and supplements. As it would be impossible to keep up with the changes, this guide uses fictitious dates and examples may not represent current law.

Official v. Unofficial Code Sets

Most jurisdictions' codes are published in more than one code set. *Bluebook* Tables 1.1 (federal) and 1.3 (states) list the code sets available in each jurisdiction. Of these multiple code sets, one set is usually the "official" code set published by, or at the request of, the jurisdiction itself. Other code sets, often called "unofficial" codes, are published by commercial publishers.

Many law firms and smaller law libraries do not maintain both official and unofficial code sets, often choosing to purchase an unofficial set because of the editorial enhancements they contain. Furthermore, the growth of online commercial databases such as LEXIS and Westlaw has many practitioners citing unofficial sets published by the database owners. To complicate matters, a growing number of states no longer publish official codes, relying on private publishers to fill the gap, further blurring the lines between official and unofficial codes.

Does it matter? Current *Bluebook* rules allow citation to any available set, although the preference is for citations to the official code. R. 12.2.1.

☞ Most practitioners cite to whichever version of the code they have at hand, official or unofficial, although local custom varies. Ask your instructor or supervisor which version you should cite.

A. Federal and State Statutes   Rules 12, B12

Statutory citations share common elements but the exact form for the citation varies by jurisdiction. This section discusses the following:

1. Determining a jurisdiction's citation form, beginning below;
2. Basic rules for federal and state citations, beginning on page 70;
3. Rules for citing code names, beginning on page 70;
4. Division of codes into titles, chapters, sections, and subsections, beginning on page 71;
5. Including publisher information, beginning on page 74; and
6. Year of code, beginning on page 75.

1. Form   Table 1

The first step in constructing a statutory citation is determining the jurisdiction's citation form in *Bluebook* Table 1.

Using Table 1 for Statutory Citation Forms

In most jurisdictions, the code is printed in more than one code set, some officially published by the state and others published by commercial publishers. The citation form differs depending on which code set you are using. Follow these steps to determine the correct form for your code set.

1. Find the jurisdiction's entry in *Bluebook* Table 1.1 (federal) or 1.3 (state).

2. Under the jurisdiction's entry, find the section titled "Statutory compilations."

3. Read the text following the Statutory compilations heading. That text will identify the "preferred" code to cite—usually the official code. Cite to this version of the code if it is available to you. Otherwise, cite to one of the other versions listed under the heading.

   ☞ Statutory compilations: Cite to Mich. Comp. Laws, if therein.

4. Immediately beneath the Statutory compilations head are two columns. The left column lists the names of all code sets available in that jurisdiction. The right column shows the citation form for each available code set. See examples, below.

Michigan Compiled Laws (1979)	MICH. COMP. LAWS § x.x (<year>)
Michigan Compiled Laws Annotated	MICH. COMP. LAWS ANN. § x.x (West <year>)
Michigan Compiled Laws Service	MICH. COMP. LAWS SERV. § x.x (LexisNexis <year>)

5. Choose the citation form for the code set you are using. Copy the citation form shown in the right column, substituting the section number for each "x" and the date in place of <year>.

Citation Form Shown in Right Column Above	Citation in Your Document
MICH. COMP. LAWS § x.x (<year>)	Mich. Comp. Laws § 446.205 (2019)
MICH. COMP. LAWS ANN. § x.x (West <year>)	Mich. Comp. Laws Ann. § 446.205 (West 2017)
MICH. COMP. LAWS SERV. § x.x (LexisNexis <year>)	Mich. Comp. Laws Serv. § 446.205 (LexisNexis 2016)

Reminder: The entries in Table 1 use SMALL CAPITALS. Practitioners may use ordinary type.

2. Basic Statutory Citations   Rules 12.1–12.3, B12.1 & Table 1

Statutory citation forms vary by jurisdiction, but generally include the following information:

(1) Name of code set being cited, abbreviated per Table 1;

(2) Section symbol and section number;

(3) Publisher, if required for the code set you are using; and

(4) Year the code set was published.

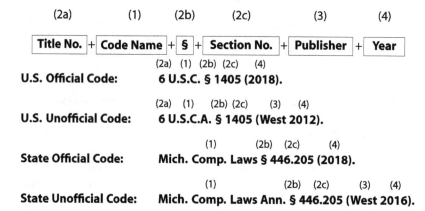

| | (2a) | (1) | (2b) | (2c) | (3) | (4) |

Title No. + **Code Name** + **§** + **Section No.** + **Publisher** + **Year**

U.S. Official Code:
(2a) (1) (2b) (2c) (4)
6 U.S.C. § 1405 (2018).

U.S. Unofficial Code:
(2a) (1) (2b) (2c) (3) (4)
6 U.S.C.A. § 1405 (West 2012).

State Official Code:
(1) (2b) (2c) (4)
Mich. Comp. Laws § 446.205 (2018).

State Unofficial Code:
(1) (2b) (2c) (3) (4)
Mich. Comp. Laws Ann. § 446.205 (West 2016).

☞ For federal statutes only: *The Bluebook* recently changed Rule 12.3.2 and no longer requires the code year be included in citations to federal statutes. See discussion on page 76 of this guide.

3. Code Name   Rule 12.3 & Table 1

Code Name + **§** + **Section No.** + **Publisher** + **Year**

- **Basic Rule No. 1: All Citations.** Include the name of the code set you are using following the form specified in Table 1 for that set.

- **Basic Rule No. 2: Citations Sentences and Clauses.** In citation sentences and clauses, abbreviate the code name as shown in Table 1.

- **Basic Rule No. 3: Embedded Citations.** When the citation is embedded in and an integral part of a text sentence, follow the appropriate rule below for the jurisdiction:

(a) **Federal Statutory Citations:** Abbreviate the name of the code as shown in Table 1.1. There is no difference between the citation sentence or embedded citation form.

(b) **State Statutory Citations:** *Do not* abbreviate any words in the name of the code set.

☞ See discussion of citation sentences, clauses, and embedded citations in Chapter 1 of this guide, beginning on page 12.

Examples: Code Name

Federal Citation Sentence	12 **U.S.C.** § 221 (2018). 12 **U.S.C.S.** § 221 (LexisNexis 2010). 12 **U.S.C.A.** § 221 (West 2011).
Federal Embedded Citation	47 **U.S.C.** § 1110 (2018) 47 **U.S.C.S.** § 1110 (LexisNexis 2010) 47 **U.S.C.A.** § 1110 (West 2011)
State Citation Sentence	**Tenn. Code Ann.** § 2-17-102 (2019). **Tenn. Code Ann.** § 2-17-102 (West 2011). **Nev. Rev. Stat.** § 40.020 (2018). **Nev. Rev. Stat. Ann.** § 40.020 (LexisNexis 2013).
State Embedded Citation	**South Carolina Code Annotated** section 23-6-30 (2019) **Connecticut General Statutes Annotated** section 5-156 (West 2012)

4. Titles, Chapters, and Section Numbers

Code sets contain all the statutes in force in a specific jurisdiction. A typical code set contains hundreds or thousands of individual statutes, divided into some combination of titles and sub-titles, parts and subparts, chapters and subchapters, etc. A few jurisdictions divide their codes by *subject matter*, discussed in Section B of this chapter. How much of this information is included in the citation depends on the individual jurisdiction. As with all statutory citations, follow the form in Table 1, including all information indicated, and matching the spacing precisely.

☞ For instructions on how to create a section symbol see the discussion and shortcuts on page 152 of this guide.

☞ Always leave a space between the section symbol and the section number, as shown here with a gray dot.

    Right: § 56-11-43   *Wrong:* §56-11-43.

- **Basic Rule No. 1: Federal Statutes.** Place the title number *before* the code name. Include a section symbol [§] after the code name, followed by the section number.

- **Basic Rule No. 2: State Statutes.** Use the state's form in Table 1.3. Place a section symbol [§] after the code name followed by the section number. A few states include the title number or chapter number either before or after the code set's name. See examples below.

  ☞ States use a variety of methods to punctuate section numbers. Some incorporate hyphens, others use periods or colons. Some states include the title number (e.g., Delaware) or chapter number (e.g., Massachusetts). Be sure to copy the form exactly as it appears in Table 1.3.

Examples: Titles and Sections

Federal Statute	6 U.S.C. **§ 1135** (2018).
State Statute (basic form)	Mont. Code Ann. **§ 7-13-2102** (West 2011).
State Statute (title)	Okla. Stat. **tit. 27, § 27-2** (2017).
State Statute (title)	3 Pa. Cons. Stat. **§ 5703** (2014).
State Statute (chapter)	Mass. Ann. Laws **ch. 267A, § 2** (LexisNexis 2019).

- **Basic Rule No. 3: Multiple Sections.** More than one section may be cited in a single citation, but the form varies depending on whether the sections are consecutive or non-consecutive. For additional information, see Chapter 1, pages 19–21 of this guide.

  (a) **Consecutive Sections:** To cite consecutive sections, use **TWO** section symbols [§§] followed by the section numbers. Separate the consecutive sections with an en dash (preferred) or a hyphen. In addition:

(1) When the statute has no internal punctuation in the section numbers, DO NOT drop repetitious digits.

Examples:

> 38 U.S.C. **§§ 1717–1718** (2018).
>
> Del. Code tit. 16, **§§ 142–143** (West 2015).

(2) When the statute has internal punctuation, drop repetitious digits preceding the punctuation.

Examples:

> Fla. Stat. **§§ 90.201–.203** (2020).
>
> La. Stat. Ann. **§§ 17:10.1–.2** (2015).

(3) When the statute's internal punctuation consists of hyphens, or in any other instance where there might be confusion, separate the sections with "to."

Examples:

> Ala. Code **§§** 27-6-7 **to -8** (2014).   ☞   *Not:* 27-6-7–8
>
> D.C. Code **§§** 39-123 **to -124** (2015)   ☞   *Not:* 39-123–124.

(b) **Non-consecutive sections:** To cite non-consecutive sections, use TWO section symbols followed by the section numbers separated by a comma. If the statute has internal punctuation, drop the repetitious digits *preceding* the punctuation, but include the last punctuation with the section number.

Examples:

> 38 U.S.C. **§§ 1717, 1719** (2018).
>
> N.C. Gen. Stat. **§§ 48-2-304, -306** (2014).

- **Basic Rule No. 4: Subsections.** To cite a subsection of a statute, append the subsection letter or number to the end of the section number, *without spaces*, and enclose in parentheses. To cite further subdivisions, append each new subsection to the end, *without spaces*, and enclose in parentheses. See examples, below.

- **Basic Rule No. 5: Multiple Subsections.** More than one subsection may be cited in a single citation, but the form varies depending on whether the subsections are *consecutive* or *non-consecutive*.

(a) **Multiple consecutive subsections:** To cite consecutive subsections of a single statute, use ONE section symbol followed by the subsection numbers separated by an en dash (strongly preferred) or a hyphen.

(b) **Multiple non-consecutive subsections:** To cite non-consecutive subsections, use ONE section symbol followed by the subsection numbers separated by a comma.

☞ For additional information on citing multiple subsections, see Chapter 1, pages 19–21 of this guide.

Examples: Sections and Subsections

Subsection	Kan. Stat. Ann. § 21-5402**(c)** (2018).
Sub-Subsection	Kan. Stat. Ann. § 21-5402**(c)(1)** (2018).
Consecutive Subsections and Sub-Subsections	Ohio Rev. Code Ann. **§ 4125.051(A)–(B)** (2019). Ohio Rev. Code Ann. **§ 4125.051(B)(1)–(3)** (2019).
Non-Consecutive Subsections and Sub-Subsections	Ohio Rev. Code Ann. **§ 4125.051(A), (C)** (West 2014). Ohio Rev. Code Ann. **§ 4125.051(B)(1), (3)** (West 2014).

☞ The consecutive sections and subsections are separated with an **en dash** instead of a hyphen in these examples. By using the wider en dash, the fact that consecutive subdivisions are cited is more noticeable.

5. Publisher   Rule 12.3.1(d)

Code Name + § + Section No. + Publisher + Year

• **Basic Rule:** Include the name of the publisher in parentheses at the end of the citation when indicated in Table 1 for the code set you are using.

☞ The publisher is included when citing *unofficial* codes. With major changes to the publication process in the last few years, the line between official and unofficial codes has blurred. The easiest thing to do is simply follow the form in Table 1 for the specific code set you are using, inserting the publisher only if indicated.

Examples: Publisher

Table 1 Entry	Your Citation
N.M. Stat. Ann. § x-x-x (<year>)	N.M. Stat. Ann. § 7-9A-5 (2019).
N.M. Stat. Ann. § x-x-x (**West** <year>)	N.M. Stat. Ann. § 7-9A-5 (**West** 2014).
N.M. Stat. Ann. § x-x-x (**LexisNexis** <year>)	N.M. Stat. Ann. § 7-9A-5 (**LexisNexis** 2016).

The first example shows the citation form for the *official code* published by Conway Greene. The second and third examples are *unofficial codes* published by West Publishing and Lexis-Nexis, respectively.

A Note About Publishers

In recent years there has been a consolidation of legal publishers. During this ongoing process, some states' hardbound code sets may identify one publisher while *Bluebook* Table 1.3 shows a different one. Or, the softbound supplement or insert (pocket part), may be published by a different company than the hardbound volume, reflecting a recent change in ownership.

☞ Always follow Table 1.3 for the correct **form** for publication information, but use the publisher's name actually appearing on the code set or supplement you are using.

---

6. Year of Code   Rule 12.3.2

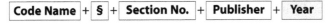

- Basic Rule: State Statutes: Include the publication year for the code set you are using, placing it in parentheses at the end of the citation. The publication year is determined by checking these places, *in the following order*:

  (1) **Spine:** If a year is printed on the spine of the book or supplement, use that date.

  (2) **Title page:** If no year appears on the spine, use the year printed on the title page.

  (3) **Copyright date:** If no year appears on the spine or title page, use the copyright year.

☞ The required information is the year that the code set was published, NOT the year the statute was enacted.

- **Basic Rule: Federal Statutes.** Inclusion of the code year is optional for federal statutes only. To include the date, follow the same procedure as for state statutes, described above. If the date is omitted, no parenthetical is necessary for citations to the official code (U.S.C.). When citing an unofficial code, include only the publisher in the parenthetical.

Examples:

U.S. Official Code:	6 U.S.C. § 1405.
U.S. Unofficial Codes:	6 U.S.C.A. § 1405 (West). 6 U.S.C.S. § 1405 (LexisNexis).

B. Additional Information in Statutory Citations

Occasionally, additional information is required for full statutory citations, or is included to help identify the statute. This section discusses the following:

1. Citing statutes printed in supplements, beginning on this page;

2. Citing subject matter codes, beginning on page 77; and

3. Citing named statutes (optional), beginning on page 77.

1. Supplements   Rule 12.3.2

- **Basic Rule:** When citing a statute that is printed in a supplement (or pocket part), include the abbreviation "Supp." in the date parenthetical. Place it after the publisher's name (if any) and before the code year.

☞ See additional discussion of citing supplements in Chapter 1 of this guide, page 24.

Examples: Supplements

Official Code: State	Va. Code Ann. § 27-3 (**Supp.** 2014).
Unofficial Code: State	Va. Code Ann. § 27-3 (West **Supp.** 2014).
Official Code: Federal	21 U.S.C. § 64 (**Supp.** 2018). *or* 21 U.S.C. § 64 (**Supp.**).
Unofficial Code: Federal	21 U.S.C.A. § 64 (West **Supp.** 2018). *or* 21 U.S.C.A. § 64 (West **Supp.**).

2. Subject Matter Codes   Rule 12.3.1(c)

- Basic Rule: Subject Matter Codes. Four states divide their codes by subject matter: California, Maryland, New York, and Texas. To cite statutes for these states, include the subject in the citation as shown in Table 1.3. Names and abbreviations for the subjects are found in the Table immediately below the state's basic form.

Examples: Subject Matter Codes

Table 1.3 Entry	Your Citation
Md. Code Ann., <Subject> § x-x (LexisNexis <year>)	Md. Code Ann., **Econ. Dev.** § 5-105 (Lexis-Nexis 2013)
Cal. <Subject> Code § x (West <year>)	Cal. **Welf. & Inst.** Code § 5840.2 (West 2014).

3. Named Statutes   Rule 10.3.1(a)

Some statutes are well known by a common name such as the Americans With Disabilities Act or Florida's Baker Act. When discussing these statutes, you may choose to include the name of the act for the convenience of your reader.

☞ If the act is not well known by its common name, or if citation to its name would not be helpful (which is true in most circumstances), do not include the statute's name in the citation.

- Basic Rule: Provide the official name of the act, placing it before the beginning of the citation. Omit "The" if it is the first word in the name. For federal statutes, include the original section number. For state statutes, include the original section number only if available. Follow the name with a comma, then the full citation following *Bluebook* rules as described in Part A of this chapter.

Examples:

Federal Statute: Homeland Security Act of 2002 § 517, 6 U.S.C. § 321f (2018).

State Statute: Nevada Fair Housing Law, Nev. Rev. Stat. Ann. § 118.020 (2017)

C. Short Forms: Statutes   Rules 4, 12.10, B12.2

- Once a statute has been cited in full, shorten subsequent references by using id. or the alternate short form described below.

1. <u>Id.</u>   Rules 4.1, 12.10, B12.2

- **Basic Rule No. 1: All <u>Id.</u> Citations.** When the immediately preceding citation is to the same section, use <u>id.</u> without a pinpoint.

- **Basic Rule No. 2: Different Subsection.** When citing a different subsection of the statute found in the immediately preceding citation, use <u>id.</u> followed by a section symbol, the section number, and the new subsection number(s) or letter(s). Do not use "at" with a section symbol.

- **Basic Rule No 3: Different Section, Same Title.** When the immediately preceding citation is to a different section found in the same title of the code, use <u>id.</u> followed by a section symbol and the new section number. Do not use "at" with a section symbol."

- **Basic Rule No 4: Different Title.** When the immediately preceding citation is to a statute found in a **different title** of the code, do not use <u>id.</u> Instead, use a full citation if the new section has not been previously cited in the document, or an alternate short short form when appropriate.

- **Basic Rule No 5: Embedded citations.** When a citation is embedded in and is an integral part of the text sentence, use an alternate short form—do not use <u>id.</u>

☞ For additional information, including when to capitalize <u>id.</u>, see the discussion of <u>id.</u> short forms beginning on page 26 of this guide.

Examples: <u>Id.</u> Short Forms

Full Citation	Wyo. Stat. Ann. § 6-3-304(a) (2018).
1. Same Section and Subsection	<u>Id.</u>
2. Same Section, New Subsection	<u>Id.</u> § 6-3-304(b). ☞ Not: <u>Id.</u> **at** § 6-3-304(b). ☞ Not: <u>Id.</u> **§ (b).**
3. Different Section, Same Title	<u>Id.</u> § 6-3-307.
4. Different Title	**Full citation:** Wyo. Stat. Ann. § 5-3-504 (2018). *or* **Alternate Short Form:** § 5-3-504 (2018).

2. Alternate Short Form   Rules 12.10, B12.2

The Bluebook provides various alternate short forms for statutory citations, but offers little information on how to choose the correct one. The discussion below will help you select an appropriate alternate short form.

- **Basic Rule:** After an intervening citation to different authority, use an alternate short form that "clearly identifies the statute" being cited. Use one of the following versions: (a) regular, (b) expanded, (c) subject matter, or (d) embedded.

  (a) **Regular alternate short form:** Include a section symbol followed by a space and the section number.

    ☞ Use a regular short form when the statute has been cited recently in your document, and there will be no confusion about the reference.

    Examples: § 152.   § 410.036.   § 14-3-16.

  (b) **Expanded alternate short form:** Add the name of the code and, if applicable, a title or chapter number, to the regular short form.

    ☞ Use an expanded form when the statute has not been cited recently in your document, or there may be confusion about the reference. For example, if your document discusses statutes from multiple jurisdictions, or you have included sections from different titles of the U.S. Code, use an expanded short form.

    Examples: 21 U.S.C. § 152.   Fla. Stat. § 410.036.   N.M. Stat. Ann. § 14-3-16.

  (c) **Subject matter alternate short form:** Add the subject matter to the regular short form.

    ☞ Use a subject matter short form when citing one of the four jurisdictions that have subject matter codes.

    Examples: Crim. Law § 2-210.   State Gov't § 20-305.

  (d) **Embedded alternate short form:** For state statutes only, spell out "section" instead of using a section symbol; do not abbreviate any words in expanded or subject matter short forms. For federal statutes, there is no difference between an embedded citation and one in a citation sentence

    ☞ Use an embedded alternate short form when the citation is an integral part of the text sentence.

  Examples: State Statutes

  section 14-3-16   Florida Statutes section 410.036   Criminal Law section 2-210

  Examples: Federal Statutes

  § 152   21 U.S.C. § 152

Examples: Short Form Statutory Citations In Context

If a minor child "living with the parents" maliciously or willfully destroys or steals property belonging to a school, the school is entitled to recover damages from the parents. [1] Fla. Stat. § 741.24(1) (2020). This rule applies to both public and private schools. [2] Id.	[1] First cite to statute; use full citation.
	[2] Same section and subsection; use id. without a pinpoint.
When parents are divorced and the child lives with one parent, application of the statute has been limited to the parent who has primary custody and control over the child. [3] Canida v. Canida, 751 So. 2d 647, 648 (Fla. Dist. Ct. App. 1999). This comports with the statutory language requiring the minor to be "living with" the parents. [4] § 741.24(1).	[3] Intervening citation to different authority.
	[4] Alternate short form after intervening citation.
To recover, the school must bring "an appropriate action at law in a court of competent jurisdiction." [5] Id. Recovery is limited to actual damages plus court costs, [6] id. § 741.24(2), and the school's recovery from the minors' parents will be offset against any amounts the school recovers as treble damages, pursuant to [7] section 812.035(7).	[5] Same section and subsection; use id. without a pinpoint.
	[6] Same section, new subsection, citation clause: use id. with section number and new subsection.
	[7] New section in same title, embedded. Alternate short form used with spelled-out "section."

Important Note

The preceding discussion covers basic statutory citation rules only. *The Bluebook* has special rules for citations to repealed statutes or prior versions of the law, an entire legislative act, individual portions of legislative acts, session laws (for uncodified acts), and named statutes published in scattered sections of the code. See *Bluebook* Rule 12 if you encounter any of these or other situations not covered by this guide.

4 Constitutions

Bluebook Whitepages Rule 11 and Bluepages Rule B11 control citation forms for Federal and state constitutions.

Constitutions are a type of enacted law but have their own citation forms. This chapter discusses the following:

A. Basic citation forms for federal and statute constitutions, below; and

B. Short forms for constitutions, beginning on page 82.

A. Basic Citation Forms   Rules 11, B11

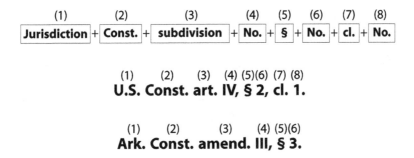

- **Basic Rule No. 1: All Constitutions.** Include the following information in the full citation:

    (1) The name of the jurisdiction, abbreviating United States to U.S. and state names according to Table 10;

    (2) The word Constitution, abbreviated to "Const.";

    (3) The word "article" or "amendment," abbreviated according to Table 16; and

    (4) The article or amendment number, written in roman numerals.

- **Basic Rule No. 2: Sections.** To pinpoint a section of the constitution, place a comma after the article or amendment number and add the following:

    (5) A section symbol, followed by a space; and

    (6) The section number, written in arabic numerals.

- **Basic Rule No. 3: Clauses.** To pinpoint a clause, place a comma after the section number and add the following:

  (7) The word clause, abbreviated as "cl."; and

  (8) The clause number, written in arabic numerals.

- **Basic Rule No. 4: Embedded Citations.** When the citation is embedded in and an integral part of a text sentence, include the same information as above, but **do not** abbreviate any words. Spell out the word "section" instead of using the section symbol.

Important Note Regarding State Constitutions

Some state constitutions vary slightly in their organization. For example, some states divide their constitutions first into chapters, then sections. Include any additional subdivisions in your citation, abbreviating as appropriate using *Bluebook* Table 16 as a guide.

B. Short Form: Constitutions   Rules 11, B11

- **Basic Rule No. 1: _Id._** If there are no intervening citations to other authority, use _id._ Include a new article, amendment, section, or clause as appropriate.

- **Basic Rule No. 2: Alternate Short Form.** If _id._ cannot be used because of intervening citations to different authority, use one of the following methods as a short form:

  (1) In citation sentences and clauses, use a full citation.

  (2) In text sentences, you may substitute the common name for the article or amendment (e.g., Fourteenth Amendment or Commerce Clause). See examples below.

Examples: Constitutions

Article	U.S. Const. art. II.
	Pa. Const. art. XII.
Amendment	U.S. Const. amend. V.
Section	U.S. Const. art. II, § 1.
	Fla. Const. art. V, § 24.

Examples continue on the next page.

Examples: Constitutions, *continued*

Clause	U.S. Const. art. II, § 1, cl. 7.	
	Cal. Const. art. IX, § 9, cl. d.	
Embedded Citations	United States Constitution article V	
	Michigan Constitution article VI, section 9	
Id. Short Form	*Same Article or Amendment*	<u>Id.</u>
	Different Article or Amendment	<u>Id.</u> amend. III.
	Same Article or Amendment, Different Section	<u>Id.</u> § 12.
	Same Article or Amendment, Different Clause	<u>Id.</u> § 12, cl. b.
Alternate Short Form	**Article VIII** gives every county the authority . . .	
	No state may deprive a person of life, liberty, or property without conforming to all **Due Process Clause** requirements.	

5 Regulations

Bluebook Whitepages Rule 14.2, Bluepages Rule B14, and Tables 1.2 and 1.3 control citations to federal and state administrative regulations. **Whitepages Rule 12.9.1** and **Bluepages Rule B12.1.4** control citations to the Internal Revenue Service Code and Treasury Regulations.

This chapter discusses citations to the following:

A. Federal administrative regulations, beginning on this page;

B. State administrative regulations, beginning on page 87;

C. Internal Revenue (IRS) code, beginning on page 88; and

D. Treasury Department regulations, beginning on page 90.

A. Federal Administrative Regulations   Rules 14.2, B14

- **Basic Rule: Code of Federal Regulations.** Cite to the Code of Federal Regulations and include the following:

  (1) The title number;

  (2) The abbreviation for Code of Federal Regulations (C.F.R.);

  (3) A section symbol (§) and the section number, including a pinpoint to subsection(s), if applicable; and

  (4) The edition year of the code set you are using, placed in parentheses at the end of the citation.

(1)		(2)		(3)		(4)
Title No.	+	C.F.R.	+	§ + Section No.	+	Year

(1) (2)   (3)   (4)
21 C.F.R. § 1302.07 (2020).

- **Basic Rule: Federal Register.** If the regulation is new and has not yet been included in the Code of Federal Regulations, cite to the Federal Register following *Bluebook* Rule 14.2(a). Include (a) the regulation's common name; (b) volume number; (c) abbreviation for Federal Register (Fed. Reg.); (d) beginning page number; (e) full date of publication, in parentheses; and (f) where the regulation will be codified, if available. See example on the next page.

- **Basic Rule: Named Regulations.** In most circumstances it is not necessary to include the name of the regulation. If including the name will be helpful because the purpose of the regulation cannot be ascertained from context, place it in front of the citation. See example below.

- **Basic Rule: Multiple Sections or Subsections.** To cite multiple sections or subsections of treasury regulations, see discussion beginning on page 19 of this guide.

- **Basic Rule: Embedded Citations.** Do not spell out words. Use a section symbol and abbreviate the Code of Federal Regulations to C.F.R.

- **Basic Rule: Short Forms.** Short forms for regulations are controlled by Rule 14.5. Use one of the following short forms:

  (1) <u>Id.</u>: If there are no intervening citations to different authority, use <u>id.</u> For additional information on <u>id.</u>, see discussion on page 26 of this guide.

  (2) **Alternate Short Form:** When <u>id.</u> cannot be used, use one of the following alternate short forms: (a) a section symbol followed by the regulation number; or (b) the title number, C.F.R. abbreviation, section symbol, and section number.

  ☞ Use version (a) if the previous citation to the regulation was recent and there will be no confusion about the reference. Otherwise, use version (b).

  ☞ Regulations change often and the code is updated frequently, thus is it important to cite to the most recent edition of the code—always double-check.

Examples: Federal Administrative Regulations

Type of Regulation	Full Citation Form	Alternate Short Form
Basic Citation to Code of Federal Regulations	10 C.F.R. § 19.12(a)(6) (2020).	§ 19.12(a)(6). *or* 10 C.F.R. § 19.12(a)(6).
Basic Citation to Federal Register	Telemarketing Sales Rule, 84 Fed. Reg. 44,687 (Aug. 27, 2019) (to be codified in 15 U.S.C. §§ 6101–6108; 15 U.S.C. §§ 6151–6155).	84 Fed. Reg. 44,687.
Named Regulation	Allocation of Budget Authority for Housing Assistance, 24 C.F.R. § 791.403 (2020).	§ 791.403. *or* 24 C.F.R. § 791.403.
Embedded Citation	15 C.F.R. § 2016.1 (2020)	§ 2016.1 *or* 15 C.F.R. § 2016.1

B. State Administrative Regulations Rules 14.2, B14

- **Basic Rule: *Bluebook* Form.** Cite regulations to the state's administrative compilation as shown in Table 1.3, using the same information included in federal regulations.

  ☞ Some states use the abbreviation "R." or "r." while others use a section symbol. Be sure to follow the state's form exactly.

- **Basic Rule: Local Form.** If a state has a local form for citing regulations, use that form in documents submitted to the jurisdiction's courts. Otherwise, use the *Bluebook* form.

- **Basic Rule: State Register.** If the regulation is new and has not yet been included in the state's official compilation, cite to the state's register, adapting the *Bluebook*'s rules for citations to the Federal Register discussed in Part A of this chapter.

- **Named Regulations.** In most circumstances it is unnecessary to include the name of the regulation. If it will be helpful to include the name because the purpose of the regulation cannot be ascertained from context, include the name by placing it in front of the basic citation. See discussion for Federal Regulations in Part A, above.

- **Basic Rule: Multiple Sections or Subsections.** To cite multiple sections or subsections of regulations, see discussion beginning on page 19 of this guide.

- **Basic Rule: Embedded Citations.** If the citation is embedded in and an integral part of the text sentence, do not abbreviate any words. Spell out "section" instead of using the section symbol.

- **Basic Rule: Short Forms.** Short forms for regulations are governed by Rule 14.4. Use one of the following short forms:

  (1) <u>Id.</u>: If there are no intervening citations to different authority, use <u>id.</u> For additional information on <u>id.</u>, see discussion on page 26 of this guide.

  (2) **Alternate Short Form:** When <u>id.</u> cannot be used, use one of the following alternate short forms: (a) a section symbol or "R." followed by the regulation number; or (b) adapt a form following the state's entry in Table 1.3. Include the shortened name of the administrative compilation followed by a second symbol or "R" and the regulation number.

     ☞ Use version (a) if the previous citation to the regulation was recent and there will be no confusion about the reference. Otherwise, use version (b).

☞ Regulations change often and codes are updated frequently, thus is it important to cite to the most recent edition of the state's code—always double-check.

Examples: State Administrative Regulations

Type of Regulation	Full Citation Form	Alternate Short Form
Michigan Administrative Code	Mich. Admin Code r. 205.402 (2020).	R. 205.402. *or* Mich. Admin. Code r. 205.402.
Maryland Code of Regulations	Md. Code Regs. 05.03.01.04 (2020).	R. 05.03.01.04. *or* Md. Regs. 05.03.01.04.
New York Codes, Rules, & Regulations	N.Y. Comp. Codes R. & Regs. tit. 13, § 200.3 (2020).	§ 200.3. *or* N.Y. Rules tit. 13, § 200.3.
Embedded Citation	25 Texas Administrative Code § 601.7 (2020)	section 601.7 *or* 25 Texas Administrative Code § 601.7

C. Internal Revenue Code   Rules 12.9.1, B12.1.4

Although citations may be made directly to the United States Code following the rules for federal statutes described in Chapter 3 of this guide, I.R.S. sections are usually cited as follows.

- **Basic Rule:** In citation sentences, clauses, and embedded citations, use ordinary type and include:

  (1) The abbreviation for the Internal Revenue Code (I.R.C.);

  (2) A section symbol (§) and the section number, including a pinpoint to any subsection(s);

  (3) Optional: When citing an unofficial code, the publisher's name in a parenthetical; and

  (4) Optional: Code year.

(1)	(2)	(3)	(4)
I.R.C.	+	§ + Section No.	+	Publisher	+	Year

	(1) (2) (4)
Official Code:	**I.R.C. § 25.2502-2 (2020).**
Or:	**I.R.C. § 25.2502-2.**

	(1) (2) (3) (4)
Unofficial Code:	**I.R.C. § 25.2502-2 (West) 2020).**
Or:	**I.R.C. § 25.2502-2 (West).**
Or:	**I.R.C. § 25.2502-2.**

♦ **Basic Rule: Optional Parenthetical.** Practitioners may omit the year and publisher parenthetical when discussing only the current version of federal tax laws. See Rule B12.1.4.

● **Basic Rule: Multiple Sections or Subsections.** To cite multiple sections or subsections of the code, see discussion beginning on page 19 of this guide.

● **Basic Rule: Embedded Citations.** Abbreviate the code name to I.R.C. and use a section symbol; do not spell out words.

● **Basic Rule: Short Forms.** Short forms for the I.R.C. Code are governed by Rule 12.10. Use one of the following short forms:

(1) <u>Id.</u>: If there are no intervening citations to different authority, use <u>id.</u> For additional information on <u>id.</u>, see discussion on page 26 of this guide.

(2) **Alternate Short Form:** When <u>id.</u> cannot be used, use one of the following alternate short forms: (a) a section symbol followed by the section number; or (b) the abbreviated name of the code (I.R.C.), a section symbol, and the section number.

☞ Use version (a) if the previous citation to the section was recent and there will be no confusion about the reference. Otherwise, use version (b).

Examples: Internal Revenue Code

Rule	Full Citation Form	Alternate Short Form
Basic Citation	I.R.C. § 5723(b).	§ 5723(b). *or* I.R.C. § 5723(b).
Embedded Citation	I.R.C. § 2501(a)(3)(B)	§ 2501(a)(3)(B) *or* I.R.C. § 2501(a)(3)(B)

D. Treasury Regulations   B12.1.4, 12.9.1, and Table 1.2

Treasury regulations are published in the Code of Federal Regulations but have their own citation form.

- **Basic Rule:** In citation sentences, clauses, and embedded citations, use ordinary type and include:

    (1) The abbreviation for Treasury Regulation (Treas. Reg.);

    (2) A section symbol (§) and the section number, including a pinpoint to any subsection(s);

    (3) Optional: When citing an unofficial code, the publisher's name in a parenthetical; and

    (4) Optional: Code year.

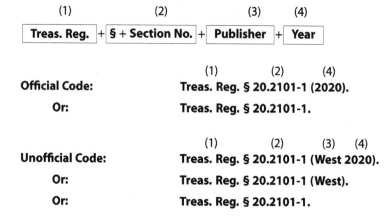

- ♦ **Basic Rule: Optional Parenthetical.** Practitioners may omit the year and publisher parenthetical when discussing only the current version of federal tax laws. See Rule B12.1.4.

- **Basic Rule: Code Year.** The code year may be included at the end of the citation but is unnecessary when citing the regulation's current version.

- **Basic Rule: Multiple Sections or Subsections.** To cite multiple sections or subsections of treasury regulations, see discussion beginning on page 19 of this guide.

- **Basic Rule: Embedded Citations.** When a treasury regulation citation is embedded in and an integral part of a text sentence, abbreviate the words and use a section symbol.

- **Basic Rule: Short Forms.** Short forms for treasury regulations are governed by Rule 12.10. Use one of the following short forms:

(1) **Id.:** If there are no intervening citations to different authority, use <u>id.</u> For additional information on <u>id.</u>, see discussion on page 26 of this guide.

(2) **Alternate Short Form:** When <u>id.</u> cannot be used, use one of the following alternate short forms: (a) a section symbol followed by the regulation number; or (b) the title, the abbreviation for Treasury Regulation, a section symbol, and the section number.

☞ Use version (a) if the previous citation to the regulation was recent and there will be no confusion about the reference. Otherwise, use version (b).

Examples: Treasury Regulations

Citation Type	Full Citation Form	Alternate Short Form
Basic Citation	Treas. Reg. § 302.1-6. *or* Treas. Reg. § 302.1-6 (West 2020).	§ 302.1-6. *or* Treas. Reg. § 302.1-6.
Embedded Citation	Treas. Reg. § 26.2652-2 *or* Treas. Reg. § 26.2652-2 (West 2020)	§ 26.2652-2 *or* Treas. Reg. § 26.2652-2

Important Note

The preceding discussion covers basic citation rules for the most frequently cited regulatory materials. *The Bluebook* has additional rules for citations to other materials, including administrative adjudications, advisory opinions, revenue rulings, presidential papers, executive orders, patents, etc. Consult *Bluebook* Rule 14 to cite these materials.

6 Procedural and Court Rules

Bluebook Whitepages Rule 12.9.3 and Bluepages Rule B12.1.3 control the form of citations to procedural and court rules.

All courts, whether federal or state, have rules of procedure regulating the conduct of business before that court. In addition, courts adopt "local rules" applicable to how business is conducted in a particular division of the courts such as trial and appellate courts, or specialized courts such as juvenile and probate divisions. This chapter discusses the following:

A. Rules of procedure and evidence, beginning on this page;

B. Court rules for federal, state, and local jurisdictions, beginning on page 95; and

C. Short form citations, beginning on page 97.

A. Rules of Procedure and Evidence   Rules 12.9.3, B12.1.3

Procedural rules govern how courts hear and determine what happens in civil, criminal, or administrative proceedings. Procedural rules may affect how evidence will be presented during trial, when an appeal can be filed, and a wide range of other matters.

1. Federal Rules of Procedure and Evidence   Rule 12.9.3

- **Basic Rule:** In citation sentences and clauses, provide the following information, in ordinary type:

  (1) The name of the jurisdiction, abbreviated to "Fed.";

  (2) The word "rule," abbreviated to "R.";

  (3) The type of rule cited, abbreviated using *Bluebook* Rule 12.9.3 as a guide; and

  (4) The specific rule number.

(1)   (2)   (3)   (4)

| Fed. | + | R. | + | Type of Rule | + | Rule Number |

(1) (2) (3)   (4)

Fed. R. Civ. P. 59

- Basic Rule: Embedded Citations. Do not abbreviate any words in the citation.

Examples: Federal Rules of Procedure and Evidence

Type of Rule	Example of Citation Form	
Rules of Civil Procedure	Fed. R. Civ. P. 12.	☞ NOT: F.R.C.P. 12.
Rules of Criminal Procedure	Fed. R. Crim. P. 28.	☞ NOT: F.R.Cr. 28.
Rules of Evidence	Fed. R. Evid. 802.	☞ NOT: F.R.E. 802.
Rules of Appellate Procedure	Fed. R. App. P. 21.	☞ NOT: F.R.A.P. 21.
Embedded Citation	According to **Federal Rule of Civil Procedure 59(b)**, a motion for new trial must be filed within twenty-eight days after entry of judgment.	

☞ **You will often see procedural rules referred to informally by using just the rule's initials, e.g., F.R.C.P., but *Bluebook* citation form requires different abbreviations. Follow the *Bluebook* form shown in the examples on the left.**

2. State Rules of Procedure and Evidence   Rules 12.9.3, B12.1.3, BT2.2

Many states have rules governing citation forms for their procedural and evidence rules. Although their abbreviations may differ, they will generally contain the same information as the *Bluebook* form. In practice you will cite using the form specified by the state where you are filing the document. If the state does not have a specific citation form, follow *Bluebook* rules, adapting the form as required. Ask your instructor or supervisor which form you should follow.

- Basic Rule: State Form. For documents filed in state courts, follow the state's citation forms. Most state forms are listed in Table BT2.2, or may be obtained from the state court's website.

- Basic Rule: *Bluebook* Form. If the state does not have a specific form or the document will be filed in a different jurisdiction, use the *Bluebook* form. Include the following information:

  (1) The name of the jurisdiction, abbreviated per Table 10.1;

  (2) The word "rule" abbreviated to "R.";

  (3) The type of rule cited, abbreviated using *Bluebook* Rule 12.9.3 as a guide; and

  (4) The specific rule number.

- Basic Rule: Embedded Citations. If the citation is embedded in and an integral part of the text sentence, do not abbreviate any words in the citation.

Examples: State Rules of Procedure and Evidence

Type of Rule	*Bluebook* Form Rule 12.9.3	State Form Table BT2.2
Idaho Rule of Evidence	Idaho R. Evid. 411(a).	I.R.E. 411(a).
Louisiana Code of Criminal Procedure	La. Code Crim. P. 262.	C.Cr.P. 262.
Ohio Rule of Civil Procedure	Ohio R. Civ. P. 21.	Civ.R. 21.
Embedded Citation: Ohio Rule of Civil Procedure	Misjoinder is not grounds for dismissal according to **Ohio Rule of Civil Procedure 21**.	Misjoinder is not grounds for dismissal according to **Civil Rule 21**.
☞ **States amend their citation rules from time to time. Verify the current form on the state's website.**		

B. Rules of Court   Rules 12.9.3, BT2.2

Rules of court govern how matters are handled and cases are processed through the court system. The rules may apply to all courts within a jurisdiction, or only specific courts. The latter are often referred to as "local rules."

☞ To find citation forms for a specific court, first check Bluepages Table 2. If you cannot find the form in BT2, use a search engine to search for [court name] + court rules. Once you have located the rules, look in the rule index for a "cite as" entry or similar terms. Often the citation form can be found in the first rule, or the last rule in the first section of rules. Many courts do not have specific citation forms; if you cannot find the local form, ask your instructor or supervisor for assistance.

1. Federal Rules of Court   Rule 12.9.3

- Basic Rule: Local Form. If the court has a specific form, use the court's form in documents filed in that court. Many citation forms for federal courts are listed in Table BT2.1, or the citation form may be obtained from the court's website.

- **Basic Rule:** *Bluebook* **Form.** If the court does not have a specific form, use the *Bluebook* form. Include the following information:

  (1) Name of court issuing the rule, abbreviated as shown in *Bluebook* Tables 7 and 10, and using ordinary type;

  (2) The word "rule" abbreviated to "R."; and

  (3) The rule number, including any applicable subsections.

- **Basic Rule: Embedded Citations.** If the citation is embedded in and an integral part of the text sentence, do not abbreviate any words in the citation.

Examples: Federal Court Rules

Court Issuing Rule	Example of *Bluebook* Form	Example of Local Form
U.S. Supreme Court	Sup. Ct. R. 34.	Same as *Bluebook* form.
Circuit Court	8th Cir. R. 27B.	Same as *Bluebook* form.
District Court	S.D. Ill. R. 83.6(a)(1).	SDIL-LR 83.6(a)(1).
Bankruptcy Court	Bankr. D. Mont. R. 4002-3.	Mont. LBR 4002-3.
District Court, Embedded Citation	**Southern District of Illinois Rule 83.1(b)** allows any licensed attorney to be admitted upon submission of a *pro hac vice* motion.	**Southern District of Illinois-Local Rule 83.1(b)** allows any licensed attorney to be admitted upon submission of a *pro hac vice* motion.

2. State Rules of Court

- **Basic Rule: State Form.** If the court has a specific form, use the court's form in documents filed in that court. Some state court forms are listed in Table BT2.2, or the citation form may be obtained from the court's website.

- **Basic Rule:** *Bluebook* **Form.** If the court does not have a specific form, use the *Bluebook* form. Using Rule 12.9.3 as a guide, include the following information:

  (1) Identity of the jurisdiction and court issuing the rule, abbreviated as shown in *Bluebook* Tables 7 and 10, and using ordinary type;

  (2) The word "rule" abbreviated to "R."; and

(3) The rule number, including any applicable subsections.

- **Basic Rule: Embedded Citations.** If the citation is embedded in and an integral part of the text sentence, do not abbreviate any words in the citation.

Examples: State Court Rules

Court Issuing Rule	Example of *Bluebook* Form	Example of Local Form
Kentucky Supreme Court	Ky. Sup. Ct. R. 3.022(c).	SCR 3.022(c).
South Carolina Family Court	S.C. Fam. Ct. R. 20.	R. 20, SCRFC.
Idaho Juvenile Court	Idaho Juv. R. 39(b).	I.J.R. 39(b).
Mississippi Unified Court Rules	Miss. Unif. Cir. & Cnty. Ct. R. 10.02	URCCC 10.02.
Nevada 7th Judicial District (From Court's Website)	Nev. 7th J. Dist. Ct. R. 4(2).	7JDCR 4(2).
Idaho Juvenile Court Embedded Citation	Pursuant to **Idaho Juvenile Rule 39(b)**, a shelter care hearing must be scheduled whenever a child is removed from the home.	Pursuant to **Idaho Juvenile Rule 39(b)**, a shelter care hearing must be scheduled whenever a child is removed from the home.

☞ **Courts amend their citation rules from time to time. Verify the current form on the state's website.**

C. Short Forms: Rules   Rule 4

The Bluebook does not provide short forms for procedural or court rules. As these rules are a type of enacted law similar to statutes, short forms should follow the general rules for statutory citations, modified as appropriate. See *Bluebook* Rule 4 (short forms), and Chapters 1 (introduction to short forms) and 3 (statutes) of this guide.

- **Basic Rule: <u>Id.</u>** To cite the same rule as the immediately preceding citation, use <u>id.</u>

- **Basic Rule: Alternate Short Form.** Use Rule 12.10 as a guide to prepare one of these suggested short forms:

(1) The abbreviation "R." followed by the rule number. Use this form only if the full citation has been used recently or it is clear from the text which rule is cited.

(2) A shortened version of the rule name following by an "R." and the rule number. Use this form if there is any possibility it may be unclear which rule is cited.

Examples: Alternate Short Forms for Rules

Rule	Suggested Short Form: *Bluebook* Form	Suggested Short Form: Local Form
Federal Rule of Evidence	R. 802. Evid. R. 802.	N/A
U.S. Supreme Court	R. 34. St. Ct. R. 34.	N/A
Kentucky Supreme Court	R. 3.022(c). Sup. Ct. R. 3.022(c).	R. 3.022(c). SCR 3.022(c).
Nevada 7th Judicial District	R. 4(2). 7th Dist. R. 4(2).	7JDCR 4(2). 7th Dist. R. 4(2).

7 Secondary Sources

Bluebook Whitepages Rules 15–16 and Bluepages Rules B15–16 control the form for citations to most secondary sources. This chapter discusses citations to the following sources:

A. Treatises and books, beginning on this page;

B. Periodicals, beginning on page 103;

C. Restatements, beginning on page 108;

D. Legal dictionaries, beginning on page 110;

E. American Law Reports (A.L.R.) annotations, beginning on page 112; and

F. Legal encyclopedias, beginning on page 114.

☞ This guide concentrates on the sources most frequently cited by practitioners. Consult *The Bluebook* if the source you are citing is not covered by this guide.

A. Treatises and Books   Rules 15, B15

- **Basic Rule: Full Citation.** Provide the following information:

    (1) Author's full name, followed by a comma;

    (2) Book title, ♦ underlined or italicized;

    (3) Pinpoint page(s) or section(s);

    (4) Publication edition, or other information if applicable; and

    (5) Year of publication.

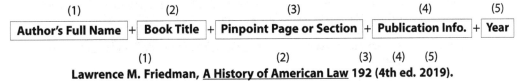

☞ Pay careful attention to comma placement. Place a comma after the author's name, but not between the book title and the page number.

☞ Small Capitals may be used for the author's name and book title. Before using Small Capitals, see discussion on page 7 of this guide.

1. Author's Full Name   Rule 15.1

- **Basic Rule: Single Author.** Provide the full name of the author, given name first, and including any designations such as Jr., Sr., etc., but not professional titles or other designations such as Prof. or J.D.

- **Basic Rule: Two Authors.** Provide the full names of both authors in the order appearing on the title page, separated by an ampersand, and following Basic Rule: Single Authors, above.

- **Basic Rule: Three or More Authors.** Use one of the following forms:

  (a) Provide the full name of the first-listed author only, followed by "et al.," which is not separated from the author's name by a comma. Follow Basic Rule: Single Authors, above, for the author's name.

      ☞ This is the preferred form.

  (b) Provide the full names of all authors in the order appearing on the title page following Basic Rule: Single Authors, above, for the authors' names. Separate the authors' names with commas, except for the last name, which should be set off with an ampersand.

      ☞ List all authors only when the authors' names are particularly relevant, a rare occurrence.

- **Basic Rule: Institutional Author.** If the author is an institution (e.g., a government agency or a non-profit organization), see *Bluebook* Rule 15.1(c). Use *Bluebook* Tables 6 and 10 for abbreviations.

Examples: Authors

Single Author	**Wayne R. LaFave**, <u>Criminal Law</u> 293 (6th ed. 2017).
Two Authors	**Jeff Koon & Andy Powell**, <u>You May Not Tie an Alligator to a Fire Hydrant: 101 Real Dumb Laws</u> 15 (2d. ed. 2002).
Three or More Authors	**Robert M. Jarvis et al.**, <u>Bush v. Gore: The Fight for Florida's Vote</u> 63–64 (2001). *or* **Robert M. Jarvis, Phyllis Coleman & Johnny C. Burris**, <u>Bush v. Gore: The Fight for Florida's Vote</u> 63–64 (2001).

2. Book Title   Rule 15.3

- **Basic Rule:** Provide the full title of the book, ♦ underlined or italicized. **Do not abbreviate** words in the title. Capitalize the first letter of each word except articles, conjunctions, and prepositions, unless they begin the title's name.

☞ Include subtitles only if particularly relevant.

☞ See examples of book titles throughout this section.

3. Pinpoint Page, Section, or Volume   Rule 3

- **Basic Rule:** Always provide the exact page or section number where the cited material appears. For additional information on pinpoints, including citing multiple pages or sections, see discussion on pages 18–21 of this guide.

Examples: Pinpoint Page or Section

Pages	Kevin A. Ewing et al., Environmental Law Handbook **182** (24th ed. 2019).
Sections	Thomas A. Dickerson, Travel Law **§ 2.07** (2005).
Volumes	**2** Austin T. Fragomen, Jr. et al., Immigration Procedures Handbook § 14:29 (2015).

☞ Notice that there is no comma between the title and the pinpoint page or section number.

4. Publication Information   Rules 15.2, 15.4

Include any applicable publication information in parentheses at the end of the citation. The following situations are the most commonly encountered by practitioners.

- **Basic Rule: Editions.** When the book has more than one edition, include the number of the edition you are citing, followed by the abbreviation "ed." for edition. If the book has only one edition, omit the edition information.

- **Basic Rule: Supplements.** To cite information found in a supplement to the main volume, include "Supp." in the parenthetical. See discussion of pinpointing supplements on page 24 of this guide.

- **Basic Rule: Editors or Translators.** When the book has an editor or translator, include that information in the parenthetical. Give (1) the editor's or translator's full name; (2) the abbreviation "ed." or "trans." as appropriate, followed by a comma to separate from other publication information in the parenthetical.

- **Basic Rule: Order of Parenthetical Information.** When including more than one piece of publication information in the parenthetical, place in the following order: (1) editors or translators, followed by a comma; (2) edition number; (3) supplement.

Examples: Publication Information

Single Edition	Jeffrey M. Gaba, <u>Environmental Law</u> 211 (2005).
Multiple Editions	Lawrence Taylor & Steven Oberman, <u>Drunk Driving Defense</u> 104(C) (8th ed. 2016).
Supplement	2 Kai Ambos, <u>Treatise on International Criminal Law</u> 230 (Supp. 2020).
Editor with Volume	2 <u>Collier on Bankruptcy</u> §302.10(3) (Alan N. Resnick & Henry J. Sommer eds., 16th ed. 2013).
Translator with Volume	1 D.A. Azuni, <u>Maritime Law of Europe</u> 116 (William Johnson trans., 2006).
Multiple Publication Information (Editor, Edition, Supplement)	Jane Q. Author, <u>How to Cite Treatises</u> 273 (John Scrivener ed., 4th ed. Supp. 2020). ☞ Notice only "editor" is set off with a comma.

☞ **For additional examples of publication information see the examples in Rule 15.2.**

5. Year   Rule 15.4

- **Basic Rule:** Include the year of publication in parentheses at the end of the citation; this will generally be the copyright year.

6. Short Forms: Treatises and Books   Rules 15.10, 4.1–.2, B15.2

- **Basic Rule:** Once a full citation has been given, a short form may be used following the rules below.

  (1) <u>Id.</u>: If there has been no intervening citation to a different authority, use <u>id.</u>, either alone or combined with a new pinpoint page, section number, or footnote number. See discussion of <u>id.</u> beginning on page 26 of this guide.

(2) **Alternate Short Form:** If there has been an intervening citation to different authority, use <u>supra</u>. Include the author's last name and a pinpoint page or section number. See discussion of <u>supra</u> beginning on page 27 of this guide.

☞ If there are two authors, use both names. If there are three or more authors, do not include all authors' names, even if all names were included in the full citation. Instead, use the first author's name followed by "et al." See examples below.

Examples: Short Forms for Treatises & Books

No intervening cite, same page or section	<u>Id.</u>
No intervening cite, new page or section	<u>Id.</u> at 135. <u>Id.</u> § 14.
After intervening cite to different authority	Dickerson, <u>supra</u>, § 4.01(4). Koon & Powell, <u>supra</u>, at 17.
After intervening cite to different authority, three authors	Jarvis et al., <u>supra</u>, at 63.

☞ Use "at" in your citation only when citing pages, never with sections.

Important Note

The preceding discussion covers basic citation rules for treatises and books. *The Bluebook* has special rules for citations to works in a collection, collected documents, and serials. Special rules apply to prefaces, forewords, introductions, epilogues, and other situations. See *Bluebook* Rule 15 if you encounter any of these situations.

B. Periodicals (Law Reviews and Journals) Rules 16, B16

This section discusses periodicals in print. Most periodicals exist in both print and online versions available in commercial databases. Cite to the print version when possible. If you are citing to a periodical that is only available through a commercial database, see Chapter 13 of this guide. If you are citing a periodical only available on the Internet (such as a law review article available on the publisher's website, see *Bluebook* rule 18.2.1 and Chapter 13.

- **Basic Rule:** Provide the following information, using ordinary type unless otherwise specified:

  (1) Author's full name, followed by a comma;

  (2) Article title, ♦ underlined or italicized, followed by a comma;

  (3) Volume number, if available;

  (4) Name of periodical, abbreviated according to *Bluebook* Tables T6, T10, and T13;

  (5) Beginning page number;

  (6) Pinpoint page(s); and

  (7) Publication year.

(1)   (2)   (3)   (4)   (5)   (6)   (7)

Author + Title + Volume + Periodical Name + Beginning Page + Pinpoint Page + Year

(1)   (2)   (3)   (4)   (5)   (6)   (7)

Alexandra Natapoff, **Misdemeanor Decriminalization,** 68 Vand. L. Rev. 1055, 1079 (2015).

1. Author's Full Name   Rule 16.2

- **Basic Rule:** Provide the full name of the author(s), given name first. Include designations such as Jr., Sr., etc.

  ☞ If there are multiple authors, follow the rules for treatises and books; see discussion beginning on page 100 of this guide.

  ☞ Occasionally a student-written work is not "signed," i.e., it does not include the author's name. In some student-written works, the author's name appears at the *end* of the piece. Always check thoroughly before concluding the work is "unsigned." To cite an unsigned work, omit the author's name but provide the rest of the citation information.

2. Article Title   Rule 16.3

- **Basic Rule: Articles.** Provide the full title of the article, ♦ underlined or italicized. Capitalize the first letter of each word except articles, conjunctions, or prepositions of less than five letters, unless it is the first word in the title. **Do not abbreviate** words in the title unless they are abbreviated in the original.

  ### *Examples:*

Less than Five Letters:	Law **in the** Age **of** Reason
Five or More Letters:	Law **in the** Age **After** Reason
Begins Title:	**Of** Law **and** Reason

- Basic Rule: Comments, Notes or Recent Developments (Student-Written Works). Cite in the same manner as other works, but include the designation of the piece (e.g., Comment, Note, Recent Development) after the author's name.

  ☞ Refer to the special rules found in *Bluebook* Rule 16.7.1 when citing to student-written works, and see the examples below.

3. Volume   Rule 16.4

- Basic Rule: Provide the volume number, if available. If the periodical has no volume number, use the publication year in place of the volume number and omit the date parenthetical from the citation.

4. Periodical Name   Rule 16.4

- Basic Rule: Provide the abbreviated name of the periodical, in ordinary type, using the abbreviations found in *Bluebook* Tables T6, T10, and T13. Follow the steps in the box below to determine the correct abbreviation.

  ☞ SMALL CAPITALS may be used for the periodical's name. Before using SMALL CAPITALS, see discussion on page 7 of this guide.

How To Abbreviate a Periodical Name

(1) Look up each word in the periodical's name in Tables **T6** (Case Names and Institutional Authors), **T10** (Geographical Terms), and **T13** (Institutional Names in Periodical Titles).
   - If the word appears in one of the tables, use the abbreviation shown.
   - If the word does not appear in any of the tables, spell out the entire word; do not abbreviate.

   ✗ **University:** When the periodical name includes University, do not abbreviate to Univ., as shown in Table T6. Instead, abbreviate as "U."

           U. Wash.   *not*   **Univ.** Wash.

(2) Omit the following words from the periodical's name: "a," "at," "in," "of," and "the" (but retain the word "on").

(3) If only one word remains in the title after "a," "at," "in," "of," or "the" have been omitted, do not abbreviate that remaining word.

(4) Check for correct spacing between abbreviations following the modified spacing rule described below.

Modified Spacing Rule for Periodical Names

Periodical names constitute an exception to the "single adjacent capital letters" rule. See *Bluebook* Rule 6.1(a) and the discussion of spacing beginning on page 24 of this guide.

- **Basic Rule: Periodicals.** Close up all adjacent single capital letters, *except when one or more of the capitals refers to the name of an institutional entity,* such as a school's law review or journal. Include a space between the entity initials and other single capital letters in the periodical's name.

    Examples:

    | N.C. ● L. ● Rev. | *not* | N.C.L. ● Rev. |
    | U.S.C. ● L.J. | *not* | U.S.C.L.J. |

---

5. Beginning Page   Rule 16.4

- Basic Rule: Provide the page number where the cited article begins.

6. Pinpoint Page(s)   Rule 3

- Basic Rule: Always provide the exact pinpoint page number(s) where the cited material appears. See discussion of pinpoints beginning on page 17 of this guide.

7. Year   Rule 16.4

- Basic Rule: Include in parentheses the year of publication. Generally this will be the copyright year. Omit months, seasons (e.g., Winter), or similar descriptions.

Short Forms: Periodicals   Rules 16.9, B16.2

- Basic Rule: Once a full citation has been given, a short form may be used following the rules below.

    1. <u>Id.</u>: If there has been no intervening citation to a different authority, use <u>id.</u>, either alone or combined with a new pinpoint page or footnote number. See discussion of <u>id.</u> beginning on page 26 of this guide.

    2. <u>Supra</u>: If there has been an intervening citation to different authority, use <u>supra</u>. Include the author's last name and a pinpoint page number. See discussion of <u>supra</u> beginning on page 27 of this guide.

☞ If there are two authors, use both names. If there are three or more authors, use the first author's name followed by "et al." Follow the same rule used for books and treatises, discussed on page 100 of this guide. See also the examples below.

Examples: Periodicals

Single Author	**Nourit Zimerman**, <u>On Individual Participation Within Mass Litigation: The Case of the Fairness Hearing</u>, 52 Akron L. Rev. 1105, 1119 (2019).
Two Authors	**Jeffrey A. Parness & Matthew Timko**, <u>De Facto Parent and Non Parent Child Support Orders</u>, 67 Am. U. L. Rev. 769, 778 (2018).
Three or More Authors	**Thomas Nadelhoffer et al.**, <u>Neuroprediction, Violence, and the Law: Setting the Stage</u>, 5 Neuroethics 67, 73 (2010).
Comment	Pamela M. Keeney, **Comment**, <u>Frozen Assets of Terrorists and Terrorist Supporters: A Proposed Solution to the Creditor Collection Problem</u>, 21 Bankr. Dev. J. 301, 328 (2004).
Note	Farrah Bara, **Note**, <u>From Memphis, with Love: A Model to Protect Protesters in the Age of Surveillance</u>, 69 Duke L.J. 197, 206–07 (2019).
Recent Development	Darpan N. Patel, **Recent Development**, <u>Not Quite 'A New HOPE'— Privacy Issues Surrounding North Carolina's New Opioid Prescription Monitoring Statute</u>, 97 N.C. L. Rev. 1828, 1833 (2019).
Short Form Citations	<u>Id.</u> *or* <u>Id.</u> at 1834. Zimerman, <u>supra</u>, at 1120. Parness & Timko, <u>supra</u>, at 779. Nadelhoffer et al., <u>supra</u>, at 75. Keeney, <u>supra</u>, at 330.

Important Note

The preceding discussion covers basic citation rules for law reviews and journals, the most frequently cited periodicals. *The Bluebook* has special rules for citations to magazines, newspapers, institutional publications, and other types of periodicals. See *Bluebook* Rule 16 if you encounter any of these situations.

C. Restatements   Rules 12.9.4, B12.1.3

- **Basic Rule No. 1: All Citations.** Provide the following information:
  (1) The word "Restatement";
  (2) Series number, if applicable, placed in parentheses;
  (3) The word "of";
  (4) Subject (e.g., Torts, Judgments, etc.), abbreviated per Table 6;
  (5) Section symbol (§);
  (6) Section number;
  (7) Name of institutional author, abbreviated per Table 6; and
  (8) Year of Publication.

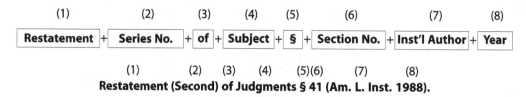

Restatement (Second) of Judgments § 41 (Am. L. Inst. 1988).

☞ The names of **institutional authors** are abbreviated using Table 6. At press time for this guide, there was an inconsistency between the print and online versions of *The Bluebook*. In the parenthetical, "Law" should be abbreviated to "L." In the print *Bluebook*, "Law" is abbreviated in the illustrations, but the online version spells it out. Although this inconsistency may have been resolved by this time, be sure to abbreviate American Law Institute to Am. L. Inst., as shown in the examples below.

☞ Don't forget to abbreviate any word in the *title* of the restatement. For example, Restatement of Contracts is abbreviated to Restatement of Conts. See examples in Rule 12.9.4 and in the table below.

- **Basic Rule No. 2: Subtitles.** For Restatements that are divided into subtitles, follow Basic Rule No. 1, but place a colon after the subject title, followed by the subtitle.

- **Basic Rule No. 3: Comments.** To cite a comment to a Restatement section, follow Basic Rule No. 1, but after the section number, insert the abbreviation "cmt." followed by the comment letter or number.

- **Basic Rule No. 4: Illustrations.** To cite an illustration of a Restatement rule, follow Basic Rules No. 1 and 3, but follow the comment number or letter with the abbreviation "illus." and the illustration number.

- **Basic Rule No. 5: Supplements.** If the cited section appears in a supplement, add "Supp." to the date parenthetical. See discussion of citing supplements on page 24 of this guide.

☞ SMALL CAPITALS may be used for the restatement name and the institution's name. Before using SMALL CAPITALS, see discussion on page 7 of this guide.

Short Forms: Restatements   Rule 4

- **Basic Rule:** Once a full citation has been given, a short form may be used following the rules below.

  (1) **Id.:** If there has been no intervening citation to a different authority, use id., either alone or combined with a new pinpoint page, section, or footnote number. See discussion of id. beginning on page 26 of this guide.

  (2) **Alternate Short Form:** If there has been an intervening citation to different authority, use an alternate short form following the general principles of short form citations for statutes found in Rule 12.10. Use one of these suggested forms:

  (a) If it will be clear to the reader the citation refers to the Restatement and not some other authority, use a section symbol followed by the pinpoint.

  (b) If the restatement has not been cited recently, or the citation may cause confusion because of other authorities cited, include the shortened name of the restatement, a section symbol, and pinpoint.

  ☞ An example of when a citation may cause confusion is when statutes and restatements are cited in the same general discussion, as both forms use section symbols and numbers.

  (c) If further clarification is required to avoid confusion, include the full name of the restatement followed by a section symbol and pinpoint.

Examples: Restatements

Full Citation	Restatement (Second) of Conts. **§ 49** (Am. L. Inst. 1981).
Supplement	Restatement (Third) of Property: Mortgages § 1.1 (Am. L. Inst. **Supp.** 2020).
Subtitle	Restatement (Third) of Torts: **Liab. for Physical Harms** § 14 (Am. L. Inst. 2005).
Comment	Restatement (Third) of Torts: Liab. for Physical Harms § 14 **cmt. c** (Am. L. Inst. 2005).
Illustration	Restatement (Second) of Agency § 220(2) **cmt. e, illus. 1** (Am. L. Inst. 1957).
Id. Short Form	Id. or Id. § 15.
Alternate Short Forms	§ 2.01. Conts. § 2.01. Restatement (Second) of Conts. § 2.01.

D. Legal Dictionaries   Rules 15.8, B15.1

- **Basic Rule:** Provide the following information:

  (1) The term being defined, *italicized* (not underlined), but see Important Note About Capitalization and Italics, below;

  (2) Dictionary name, with no abbreviations, ♦ underlined or *italicized*;

  (3) Edition number, if any; and

  (4) Year of publication.

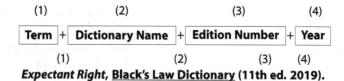

Expectant Right, Black's Law Dictionary (11th ed. 2019).

- ☞ SMALL CAPITALS may be used for the book title. Before using SMALL CAPITALS, see discussion on page 7 of this guide.

Important Note About Italics Capitalization

Capitalization: *Bluebook* rules 15.8 and B15.1 are inconsistent when the defined term includes two or more words. In the first example in Whitepages rule 15.8, Noscitur a sociis, only the first word is capitalized. In the example immediately below it, Good-Faith Bargaining, the term bargaining is capitalized as well as the first term. In the Bluepages, only the Good-Faith Bargaining example appears. Should you capitalize the second word? As a practitioner, follow the Bluepages example with its capitalized second term.

Italics: Bluepages rule B15.1 shows mixed typefaces—both italics and underlining in the same citation. Traditionalists might say that mixing the typefaces is "wrong," and that they should be both italics or both underlining. For those using underlining in their citations, go ahead and mix the typefaces as shown in Bluepages rule 15.1. For those using italics in citations, use italics for both the defined term and the dictionary title.

Short Forms: Dictionaries   Rule 15.10

☞ *The Bluebook* does not provide short forms specific to dictionaries. The citation form for dictionaries contains no pinpoint page or section number, making it different from a typical short form for books illustrated in Rule 15.10. The following are suggested short forms for dictionaries. See general discussion of short form citations beginning on page 26 of this guide.

- **Basic Rule:** Once a full citation has been given, a short form may be used following the suggestions below.

    (a) <u>Id.</u>: If there is no intervening cite to different authority, use <u>id.</u> to cite the same definition. To cite a different definition from the same dictionary, use alternate short form (c), below.

    (b) **Alternate Short Form: Same Definition.** If there has been an intervening citation to different authority, include the dictionary's name, shortened, followed by a comma and the word <u>supra</u>. No pinpoint is necessary

    (c) **Alternate Short Form: Different Definition.** To cite a *different* definition from the same dictionary previously cited, include the defined term, in italics, followed by the shortened name of the dictionary, then <u>supra</u>. No pinpoint is necessary.

- **Basic Rule: All Citations.** Provide the following information:

    (1) Author's full name including designations such as Jr. or III, but omitting terms such as Prof. or J.D., followed by a comma;

    (2) The word "Annotation," followed by a comma;

    (3) Title of the annotation, ♦ underlined or italicized, with no abbreviations. Capitalize the first letter of each word except articles, conjunctions, and prepositions, followed by a comma;

    (4) Volume number;

Examples: Dictionaries

Full Citation	*Donee Beneficiary*, <u>Barron's Law Dictionary</u> (7th ed. 2016). *Successeurs,* <u>Dahl's Law Dictionary/Dictionnaire Juridique Dahl</u> (3d ed. 2007).
Short Form	(a) <u>Id.</u> (b) <u>Barron's</u>, <u>supra</u>. (c) *Primary Beneficiary,* <u>Barron's</u>, <u>supra</u>.

E. American Law Reports (A.L.R.) Annotations   Rule 16.7.6

American Law Reports has introduced two new series: A.L.R. 7th (state law annotations) and A.L.R. Fed. 3d (federal annotations). Starting with these new series, A.L.R. began organizing annotations by article number. *The Bluebook* updated its citation form to reflect the change and to omit the beginning page number from citations to the new series.

The Bluebook includes a citation example for the new series, but not for the older series still in use by practitioners (state 3d through 6th, Fed., and Fed. 2d). The discussion below provides citation forms for both the new and older series.

(5) Abbreviation for American Law Reports ["A.L.R."], followed by the series number [e.g., 5th, 7th, Fed. or Fed. 3d];

(6) The (a) beginning page number (older series); or (b) article number (new series);

(7) Pinpoint page number; and

(8) Year of publication.

(1)	(2)	(3)	(4)	(5)	(6)	(7)	(8)
Author	"Annotation"	Title	Vol.	A.L.R. & Series	(a) Beginning Pg. or (b) Art. No.	Pinpoint	Year

            (1)   (2)   (3)   (4)   (5) (6) (7) (8)
(a) George L. Blum, Annotation, <u>Religion as a Factor in Child Custody Cases</u>, 124 A.L.R.5th 203, 212 (2004).

            (1)   (2)   (3)   (4)   (5)   (6) (7) (8)
(b) Christine Bacon, Annotation, <u>What Constitutes Fair Use of Internet Materials</u>, 5 A.L.R. Fed. 3d Art. 6, 471 (2015).

☞ **Supplement:** If the cited information appears in a supplement, include the abbreviation "Supp." in the end parenthetical. See discussion of supplements beginning on page 24 of this guide.

☞ **No Author:** If the annotation has no author, begin the citation with the word "Annotation," followed by the remaining citation information.

☞ **Multiple Authors:** If the annotation has multiple authors, see discussion of multiple authors for books beginning on page 100 of this guide.

☞ **Multiple Pages:** To cite multiple pages, see discussion beginning on page 18 of this guide.

Short Forms: A.L.R. Annotations   Rule 16.9

- **Basic Rule:** Once a full citation has been given, a short form may be used following the rules below.

  (1) **Id.:** If there has been no intervening citation to a different authority, use id., either alone or combined with a new pinpoint page, section number, or footnote number. See discussion of id. beginning on page 26 of this guide.

  (2) **Alternate Short Form:** If there has been an intervening citation to different authority, use supra. Include the author's last name and a pinpoint page number. See discussion of supra beginning on page 27 of this guide.

  ☞ If there are two authors, use both names separated by an ampersand. If there are three or more authors, use the first author's name followed by "et al." See examples below.

Examples: Annotations

Federal Series	**(a)**	Jason Binimow, Annotation, Designation as Unlawful or Enemy Combatant, 185 **A.L.R. Fed.** 475, 490 (2003).
	(b)	Eric C. Surette, Annotation, First Amendment Protection for School Principals Subject to Demotion, Transfer, or Reassignment Because of Speech, 4 **A.L.R. Fed. 3d** Art. 5, 279 (2015).
State Series	**(a)**	Randy J. Sutton, Annotation, Products Liability: Paints, Stains, and Similar Products, 69 **A.L.R.5th** 131, 139 (1999).
	(b)	Kimberly J. Winbush, Annotation, Admissibility of Victim Impact Evidence in Noncapital State Proceedings, 8 **A.L.R.7th** Art. 6, 411 (2016).
No Author		**Annotation**, Products Liability: Personal Injury or Death Allegedly Caused by Defect in Steering System in Motor Vehicle, 100 A.L.R.3d 158, 169 (1980).
Short Forms		Id. Id. at 124. Jimenez, supra, at 92–93. Parker & Buckman, supra, at 401. Fischer et al, supra, at 384.

☞ Notice in the federal series there are spaces between A.L.R., Fed., and the series number: A.L.R. · Fed. · 3d. In the state law series, there are no spaces: A.L.R.6th. See the spacing rules on page 24 of this guide.

F. Legal Encyclopedias   Rule 15.8

- **Basic Rule: All Citations.** Provide the following information:

  (1) Volume number;

  (2) Abbreviated name of encyclopedia and series number, if applicable;

  (3) Title of *main* article or entry, without abbreviations, ♦ underlined or italicized;

  (4) Section symbol (§);

  (5) Section number; and

  (6) Year of publication.

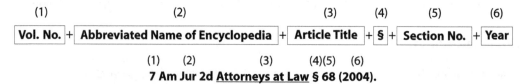

7 Am Jur 2d <u>Attorneys at Law</u> § 68 (2004).

☞ **Supplement:** If the cited information appears in a supplement, include the abbreviation "Supp." in the parenthetical. See discussion beginning on page 24 of this guide.

☞ **Multiple Sections:** To cite to multiple sections, see discussion beginning on page 19 of this guide.

☞ **Subsections:** To cite subsections, see discussion beginning on page 19 of this guide.

☞ SMALL CAPITALS may be used for the book title. Before using SMALL CAPITALS, see discussion on page 7 of this guide.

Short Forms: Encyclopedias   Rule 15.10

- **Basic Rule:** Once a full citation has been given, a short form may be used following the rules below.

  1. <u>Id.</u>: If there has been no intervening citation to a different authority, use <u>id.</u>, either alone or combined with a new pinpoint page, section number, or footnote number. See discussion of <u>id.</u> beginning on page 26 of this guide.

  2. **Alternate Short Form:** If there has been an intervening citation to different authority, use <u>supra</u>. Include the volume number, abbreviated name of the encyclopedia, and a pinpoint page or section number. See discussion of <u>supra</u> beginning on page 27 of this guide.

Examples: Encyclopedias

Encyclopedia	Example of Citation
American Jurisprudence	17 Am. Jur. 2d <u>Contracts</u> § 441 (2012).
Corpus Juris Secundum	60 C.J.S. <u>Motor Vehicles</u> §§ 50, 52 (Supp. 2019). ☞ Notice the two section symbols used to pinpoint multiple sections.
State Encyclopedias	7 Fla. Jur. <u>Boats, Ships, and Shipping</u> § 53 (2004). 1 Ohio Jur. <u>Abandoned, Lost, and Escheated Property</u> § 2 (2003). 2 N.Y. Jur. <u>Administrative Law</u> § 118 (2003). ☞ Follow the general form for citations to Am. Jur. or C.J.S., changing the encyclopedia name as appropriate. Use *Bluebook* Table 10 for abbreviations.
Short Forms	<u>Id.</u> <u>Id.</u> § 517. 32 Am. Jur. 2d, <u>supra,</u> § 27.

Important Note

The preceding discussion covers basic citation rules for the most frequently cited secondary sources. Check the index in the *Bluebook* for citation rules for sources not addressed by this guide.

8 Litigation Documents and Record Citations

Bluebook Bluepages Rule B17 controls the form for citations to documents filed in trial courts (litigation documents) and citations to the record in appellate courts.

In documents submitted to trial courts, it may be necessary to refer to other documents previously submitted that are a part of the court file. These are collectively referred to as "litigation documents." If a case is in the appellate stage, an official record of the proceedings in the lower court is created called the "record on appeal," or simply the "record." Citations to both litigation documents and the appellate record are almost exclusively used by practitioners, thus the special rules that apply to these citations are found in the Bluepages.

This chapter discusses the following:

A. Basic citation forms for litigation documents and record citations, beginning on this page;

B. Short forms for litigation documents, beginning on page 120; and

C. Enclosing citations in parentheses (optional), beginning on page 121.

A. Litigation Documents and Appellate Record   Rule B17

- **Basic Rule:** To cite a litigation document or the appellate record, provide the following information. ♦ The entire citation may be placed in parentheses; see the Note on the next page.

(1) Title of the document, abbreviated if appropriate; and

(2) Pinpoint to the exact page, line, paragraph or section of the document.

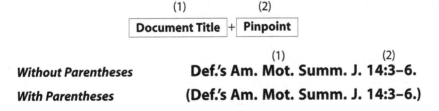

	(1)	(2)
Without Parentheses	**Def.'s Am. Mot. Summ. J. 14:3–6.**	
With Parentheses	**(Def.'s Am. Mot. Summ. J. 14:3–6.)**	

♦ Important Note About Using Parentheses

By tradition and long-standing *Bluebook* rules, citations to court documents have been enclosed in parentheses, but many jurisdictions have abandoned those parentheses. This guide uses the "modern" form — without parentheses, but ask your instructor or supervisor whether parentheses should be used for your litigation document citations. If parentheses are used, see Part C of this chapter, on page 117.

---

1. Document Title   Rule B17.1.1

- **Basic Rule No. 1: Title.** Provide the title of the document, abbreviated according to Bluepages Table BT1. Omit articles and prepositions unless the result would be ambiguous.

  ☞ If a word of seven or more letters is not listed in Table BT1, you may use a well-known abbreviation as long as the result is unambiguous. When in doubt, spell it out.

     Example: **Disposition** Hearing   ☞   **Dispo.** Hr'g

- **Basic Rule No. 2: Appellate Records.** An appellate record may be known by different names depending on the jurisdiction, but in citations it is always referred to as the "Record" and is abbreviated as "R."

- **Basic Rule No. 3: Multiple Documents with Same Title.** If the litigation or court file contains multiple documents with the same title, include additional identifying information as follows:

  (a) **Name:** For depositions, affidavits, letters, or similar documents given by or identified with a person, include the person's name by placing it before the document's title. Use only the surname name if it sufficiently identifies the person. Use the full name if necessary to distinguish parties (e.g., a husband and wife are both parties to the action). See example (a), below.

  (b) **Date:** Include the document's date. Place the date at the end of the citation separated by a comma. Abbreviate months according to Table 12. See example (b), below, and *Bluebook* Rule B17.1.3.

  (c) **Name and Date:** When necessary, use both name and date. See example (c), below.

  (d) **Other Identifying Information:** If using the above methods does not sufficiently distinguish the document from other similar documents, add additional information. This may be a nickname, time of day, or a numbering system you have assigned. You will likely need to identify your naming convention in the text of the document. See example (d), below.

- **Basic Rule No. 4: Embedded Citations.** Do not abbreviate any words in the title if the citation is embedded in and an integral part of a text sentence.

Examples: Document Titles

Basic Form	Req. Reh'g Def.'s Mot. Summ. J.
Appellate Records	R. at 1248–52.
Multiple Documents with Same Title	(a) **Armstrong** Dep. *or* **Louise Chen** Dep. (b) Aff., **Apr. 6, 2014.** (c) **Foster** Decl., **Jan. 16, 2015.** (d) **Smoking Gun E-mail** (using nickname for document)
Embedded Citations	Request for Rehearing Defendant's Motion for Summary Judgment Record Armstrong Deposition

2. Pinpoint Citations   Rule B17.1.2

- **Basic Rule:** Include a pinpoint cite to the exact place the cited material appears, following the specific rules below to cite to pages, sections, paragraphs, lines, or exhibits.

    (a) **Pages: Litigation Documents.** If the document is divided into pages, provide the page number(s) after the document title; DO NOT use "at" to separate the title and page number. For single page documents, pinpoint to page 1.

    (b) **Pages: Appellate Record.** To cite the appellate record, provide the page number(s) after the document title, preceded by the word "at."

    (c) **Sections:** If a document is divided into sections, insert a section symbol (§), followed by a space and the section number.

    (d) **Paragraphs:** If a document is divided into numbered paragraphs, insert a paragraph symbol (¶), followed by a space and the paragraph number.

    (e) **Lines:** If the document further divides pages into numbered lines, provide the page number on which the lines appear, followed by a colon and the specific line numbers.

    (f) **Exhibits:** If the material you are citing is in an exhibit or appendix attached to the document, include the abbreviation "Ex." (for Exhibit) or "App." (for Appendix) after the document title, followed by the exhibit or appendix name.

☞ To cite multiple pages, sections, paragraphs, or lines, see discussion beginning on page 17 of this guide.

☞ For subdivisions not listed above, see *Bluebook* Table 16, which includes abbreviations for columns, schedules, tables, and other terms you may encounter, allowing for more precise pinpointing. Also consult Rule 17.1.2.

Examples: Pinpoint Citations

Subdivision	Document	Citation
Page	Plaintiff's Reply Brief, page 3.	Pl.'s Reply Br. **3**.
Record	Appellate Record, page 1102.	R. **at** 1102.
Section	Contract, section 15.	Contract **§ 15**.
Paragraph	Eastern Affidavit, paragraph 29.	Eastern Aff. **¶ 29**.
	Western Affidavit, paragraphs 26 and 27.	Western Aff. **¶¶ 26–27**.
Lines	Taft Deposition, page 86, lines 18 through 22.	Taft Dep. **86:18–22**.
	Taft Deposition, page 97, line 23, through page 98, line 4.	Taft Dep. **97:23–98:4**.
Exhibit or Appendix	Parson Complaint, Exhibit A	Parson Compl. Ex. A, 3.
	Drury Application, Appendix 3, paragraph 6	Drury Appl. App. 3, ¶ 6.

☞ Notice that cites to the Record are the only time the word "at" is used.

☞ Include a space between the section or paragraph symbol and the section or paragraph number.

☞ See additional examples of pinpoint citations in Bluepages Rule B17.1.2.

B. Short Forms: Litigation and Record Citations   Rule B17.2

- **Basic Rule:** After a full citation has been given, for subsequent references use a short form that will clearly convey to the reader which document is being cited. <u>Id.</u> may be used, if appropriate, or a shortened version of the full citation.

☞ See discussion of short form citations beginning on page 26 of this guide, and examples below and in *Bluebook* Rule B17.2.

✗ Exception for the Appellate Record: When citing an appellate record, only use id. when citing the *same page*. When citing a different page, use R. at xx.

Examples: Short Form Litigation & Record Citations

Type of Document Cited	Id. Short Form	Alternate Short Form
Litigation Document	Id. Id. **at** 136. Id. § 15.	Pl.'s Reply ¶¶ 7, 13. Pet. 3–4.
Appellate Record	Id. R. **at** 1103.	R. **at** 557.
☞ Notice **"at"** is used only for citations to pages.		

C. Enclosing Citations in Parentheses

When local custom or your supervisor requires parentheses around litigation document and record citations, you will need to adjust the punctuation as described below.

• **Basic Rule: Punctuation.** Place punctuation inside or outside the closing parenthesis according to the following rules:

(a) **Citation Sentences:** Include the final period INSIDE the closing parenthesis when the citation is in a citation sentence.

(b) **Citation Clauses and Embedded Citations:** Place punctuation outside the closing parenthesis.

(1) When the citation appears at the *end* of your sentence, place a period outside of the closing parenthesis as final punctuation.

(2) When the citation is in a clause in the *middle* of your sentence, do not place any punctuation inside the closing parenthesis. Do not set off a citation clause with commas, although you should include a comma after the citation if required by ordinary rules of grammar.

Examples: Punctuation When Parentheses Are Used with Litigation Document Citations

The Plaintiff initially claimed that he did not know that the Defendant was nearby [1] **(Compl. 26)** and that he "never saw what hit him" [2] **(Johnson Dep. 79:15–16),** but he later contradicted himself [3] **(Johnson Aff. 18).** Furthermore, a witness stated that the Plaintiff taunted the Defendant just before the Defendant struck the Plaintiff with the garbage can lid. [4] **(Tyne Aff. 9.)** The police report sheds no light on what might have been said between the parties because the police arrived after the incident was over and did not interview any witnesses. [5] **(Decl. ¶ 5, Oct. 12, 2014.)**	[1] **Mid-Sentence Citation Clause:** No punctuation. [2] **Mid-Sentence Citation Clause:** Comma included after citation to punctuate independent clause. [3] **Sentence-Ending Citation Clause:** No comma, but sentence-ending punctuation placed after the parenthesis. [4] **Citation Sentence:** Period placed inside parenthesis. [5] **Citation Sentence:** Period placed inside parenthesis.

9 Strings, Signals, and Explanatory Parentheticals

Bluebook Whitepages Rules 1.2–1.5 and Bluepages Rule B1 control the form for string citations, signals and explanatory parentheticals—tools used to concisely convey information about authorities without a detailed discussion. These tools can be used individually or combined as appropriate. This chapter discusses the following:

A. String citations, beginning on this page;

B. Signals, beginning on page 126; and

C. Explanatory parentheticals, beginning on page 131.

A. String Citations   Rules 1.1, 1.4, B1.1

A string citation is two or more authorities that appear one after another to support a single proposition. The basic rules for string citations are discussed in Part 1 of this section, and short forms in string citations are discussed in Part 2.

> **Example: Two cases in a string citation**
>
> An appellate court may use a different rationale than the district court as long as the ground is supported by the record. **Lahoti v. VeriCheck, Inc.,** 586 F.3d 1190, 1196 (9th Cir. 2009); **Lambert v. Blodgett,** 393 F.3d 943, 965 (9th Cir. 2004).

1. String Basics

- **Basic Rule: All String Citations.** Prepare a citation for each authority included in the string citation following *Bluebook* rules for that authority. Arrange the authorities within the string in a logical manner: If one authority is considerably more helpful or authoritative than another, it should precede the other, less helpful or authoritative ones. Separate individual authorities with semicolons.

☞ Although *The Bluebook* may show examples of multiple authorities contained in a single string, practitioners should think carefully before using more than two. Long string citations are difficult to read and obscure your point.

About "Logical Manner"

Arranging authorities in a logical manner is new to the 21st edition of *The Bluebook*. The previous edition followed a strict, traditional order based on the hierarchy of each type of authority (statute, case, treatise, etc.). The new rule leaves it up to you to determine how to arrange the authorities in the string citation. There is no right way to order authorities as it will depend upon your issues, but here are some hints.

☞ Always place binding authority first.

☞ If your issue is controlled by the law of a particular jurisdiction (e.g., State *X*, or 10th Circuit), the controlling jurisdiction's authorities should be listed first as they are more authoritative, followed by authorities from other jurisdictions.

Example: Controlling jurisdiction is Illinois

Nat'l Bank of Bloomington v. Norfolk & W.R. Co., 383 N.E.2d 919, 923 (Ill. 1978); Evans v. Gibson, 31 P.2d 389, 392 (Cal. 1934).

☞ If your issue is controlled by enacted law (e.g., constitutions or statutes), list the enacted law first, then any supporting cases.

Example: Controlling authority is a statute

28 U.S.C. § 2244(d)(1); Morris v. Horn, 187 F.3d 333, 337 (3d Cir. 1999).

☞ If two or more cases from the same jurisdiction state the same proposition, list the cases from the highest court first, followed by lower courts. If the cases are from the same jurisdiction and court, arrange them in reverse chronological order.

Examples: Multiple authorities of same type

Different Court Levels: People v. Avila, 208 P.3d 634, 645 (Cal. 2009); People v. Johnson, 35 Cal. App. 5th 134, 137 (2019).

Same Court, Reverse Chronological Order: Whitney v. Guys, Inc., 826 F.3d 1074, 1076 (8th Cir. 2016); Hitt v. Harsco Corp., 356 F.3d 920, 923 (8th Cir. 2004).

☞ Still in doubt? Follow the hierarchy of authority using the traditional method, arranging authorities in the order shown below.

Traditional Order of Authorities in a String Citation

When citing multiple authorities in a string citation, the traditional method is to organize authorities by hierarchy, in the order shown below. For example, the [1] Federal Constitution is the highest law of the land and is placed first, while a [12] law review article is the least authoritative and is placed last.

1. Federal Constitution	7. Federal district court cases
2. State constitutions	8. Other federal court cases
3. Federal statutes	9. State court cases
4. State statutes	10. Restatements
5. U.S. Supreme Court cases	11. Books & treatises
6. Federal circuit court of appeals cases	12. Law review and journal articles

Example: A citation to the [1] Federal Constitution; a [3] federal statute; and a [4] state case, would be written as:

U.S. Const. art. VI, § 2; 8 U.S.C. § 1621 (2018); In re Garcia, 58 Cal. 4th 440, 459–60 (2014).

2. Short Forms in String Citations   Rule 4

- **Basic Rule.** Short forms may be used in string citations—with caution—for any authority that has previously been cited in full, following the short form rules for the authority being cited. **Before using the id. short form, see the exception below.**

✗ **Exception for Id.:** When the immediately preceding citation contains more than one authority, id. cannot be used. In other words, when the immediately preceding citation is a string citation, use an alternate short form for the new citation.

☞ Why? It would not be clear to the reader which authority the id. referred to in the previous string citation. One authority? All cited authorities?

Examples:

First Citation:	Ky. Rev. Stat. Ann. § 156.029 (2018); Tenn. Code Ann. § 49-1-301 (2020).
Next Citation:	§ 156.029.
Or:	Ky. Rev. Stat. Ann. § 156.029.
But not:	Id.

Examples: Short Forms in String Citations

A court may grant habeas relief if a state court decision was "contrary to" clearly established federal law. **Ferrell v. Hall, 640 F. 3d 1199, 1223 (11th Cir. 2011).** A state court decision is "contrary to" clearly established law if the court arrived at a conclusion opposite to the one reached by the Supreme Court on a question of law. **Id. at 1223; Williams v. Taylor, 529 U.S. 362, 405 (2000).**	First citation contains single authority. Id. used because previous citation contained only one authority.
Class certification of unfair competition claims is available only to those class members who were actually exposed to the business practices at issue. **Berger v. Home Depot USA, Inc., 741 F.3d 1061, 1068 (9th Cir. 2014); Mazza v. Am. Honda Motor Co., 666 F.3d 581, 595-96 (9th Cir. 2012).** It must be reasonable to presume that all class members were exposed to the misleading statements. **Berger, 741 F.3d at 1068; Mazza, 666 F.3d at 586.**	First citation contains two authorities. Alternate short form used because previous citation contains two authorities.

B. Signals   Rules 1.2–1.4, B1.2

A signal is a word or brief phrase placed in front of a citation to indicate how the cited authority relates to a proposition stated in the text. This section discusses:

1. Signal Basics, starting on page 127;

2. Using multiple signals in string citations, beginning on page 129;

3. Using signals with short forms, beginning on page 131, and

4. Using signals with explanatory parentheticals, beginning on page 131.

The Bluebook authorizes eleven signals, plus combination signals. Practitioners typically use only six of these signals, the ones that indicate support or provide background information. The remaining signals, used for making comparisons or showing contradiction, are more commonly used by academic writers.

Signals must be chosen with care because each conveys a slightly different message to the reader. The six support and background signals commonly used by practitioners are described in Chart A, below. For explanations of other signals, see *Bluebook* Rule 1.2.

1. Signal Basics

- **Basic Rule: All Signals.** Determine the appropriate signal by using Chart A, below, and the descriptions in *Bluebook* rule 1.2. Once the appropriate signal has been identified, place it before the citation. ◆ Underline or *italicize* the signal. Capitalize the signal only if it begins a citation sentence.

    Examples:

    Underlining: See also Stone v. State, 74 S.W.3d 591, 594 (Ark. 2001).

    Italics: *See also Stone v. State, 74 S.W.3d 591, 594 (Ark. 2001).*

☞ When signals are used with *cases*, both the signal and the case name must be underlined or italicized. Keep these two things in mind:

  - Be consistent. If you underline the signal, underline the case name; if you use italics, italicize both.

  - If you use underlining, **break the underline** between the signal and case name; do not use one continuous line to underline both. Notice the break in the example above.

- **Basic Rule: Combining Signals.** Signals can be combined when appropriate. ◆ Underline or *italicize* as one unit.

    Example: See + E.g., = See, e.g.,

    Merely moving into a home with another with whom one has a romantic relationship does not constitute the giving of consideration essential to contract formation. **See, e.g.,** Williams v. Ormsby, 131 Ohio St. 3d 427, 437 (2012).

Chart A: Description of Individual Signals

Signal Name	When to Use This Signal	Comments
[No Signal]	The authority directly states the proposition.	Used when the proposition is a quote or close paraphrase of the authority.
E.g.,	Multiple authorities state the proposition but only this authority is cited.	When multiple authorities state the same proposition, it is rarely necessary to cite them all. Use the e.g. signal followed by citations to one or two of the "best" authorities.

Chart continues on the next page.

Chart A: Description of Individual Signals, *continued*

Signal Name	When to Use This Signal	Comments
Accord	More than one authority states or clearly supports the proposition but the text only discusses one of them.	Most commonly used in string citations to show that prior cases in the same jurisdiction, or the law of another jurisdiction, states the same proposition.
See	The authority supports but does not directly state the proposition. Often referred to as "inferential" or "indirect" support.	Using see advises the reader that an inferential step must be taken between the proposition and the citation.
See also	Cited authority supports the proposition but will not be discussed.	Primarily used in string citations when other authority directly supports the proposition. Use an explanatory parenthetical to show why the authority is relevant.
See generally	Cited authority gives background information that may be helpful but will not be discussed.	Often used in connection with a well-known legal rule or proposition. The writer first cites the proposition to one authority, then cites (but does not discuss) additional authority using see generally.

A Note About Direct v. Inferential Support

Pay careful attention to whether a citation "directly" or "inferentially" supports your proposition so that you can choose the correct signal.

Direct Support: The cited portion of the authority matches what your proposition says. It may be a quotation or a paraphrase, but it will be evident to the reader how the authority supports the proposition.

Inferential Support: The cited portion of the authority does not say precisely what your proposition says, but is analogous or follows from it. The reader must take an inferential step to "see" how the authority supports the proposition.

2. Using Multiple Signals in a Single String   Rules 1.3, 1.4

Signals may be used with multiple authorities in a string citation. All authorities may follow the same signal, or multiple signals may be used when appropriate. Read the inset below, About Type and Rank, then follow the steps to correctly order your signals and authorities in a string citation:

About Type and Rank

Type: There are four "types" of signals: Support, comparison, contradiction, and background. The right column in Chart B, below, briefly describes each signal type. Notice in the chart that individual signals are grouped by signal *type*, and are arranged in a hierarchy: Support-type signals at the top, as they provide the strongest support for your proposition, and the background-type signal at the bottom, as they provide the weakest support. Signal types factor into your citation in Step 4, below.

Rank: Within each signal type, individual signals are "ranked." Chart B assigns a number to each signal. A signal ranked 2. offers more authority than a signal ranked 8.

Step 1: After determining the appropriate signal for each authority you will include in your string citation, use Chart B, below, to determine the signal's "rank."

Chart B: Signal Types and Ranks

Signal Types	Individual Signals and Their Ranks	Description of Signal Types
Support	1. [No signal] 2. E.g., 3. Accord 4. See 5. See also 6. Cf.	Cited authority directly or indirectly supports the proposition in the text.
Comparison	7. Compare	Cited authority either supports or illustrates the proposition, with the actual comparison made in an explanatory parenthetical.
Contradiction	8. Contra 9. But see 10. But cf.	Cited authority directly or indirectly supports a proposition *contrary to* the proposition in the text.
Background	11. See generally	Cited authority provides background information about the proposition.

Step 2: Arrange authorities in your string by **rank order,** as identified in Chart B.

☞ Notice that each signal is "ranked" with a number. The higher the number, the stronger the support it offers.

Step 3: If multiple authorities share the same signal, arrange the authorities within the string in a logical manner as discussed in section A of this chapter.

Step 4: Separate individual authorities in the string with appropriate punctuation following these rules:

(a) Separate individual authorities of the **same type** with **semicolons.**

(b) Separate individual authorities of **different types** with **periods.**

☞ In other words, each *type* of signal (and its authorities) is in it its own citation sentence, starting with a capital letter and ending in a period. Each *new type* of signal added to the string begins a new citation sentence. See the examples, below.

Examples: Multiple Signals with Multiple Authorities

A court may exercise its discretion in determining if a prisoner has sufficient cause to excuse a procedural default. [1] **See** McCleskey v. Zant, 499 U.S. 467, 490 (1991); [2] **see also** Coleman v. Thompson, 501 U.S. 722, 730-31 (1991). Default is excused only when a prisoner is "impeded or obstructed in complying with the State's established procedures . . . ." [3] Martinez v. Ryan, 132 S. Ct. 1309, 1318 (2012). [4] **See generally** Reed v. Ross, 468 US 1, 16 (1984) (holding claim's novelty excused attorney's failure to timely raise issue).	***The first sentence*** of this passage is supported by cases [1] and [2] using the support-type signals <u>see</u> and <u>see also</u>. **Case [1]:** The <u>see</u> signal ranks higher in Chart B than other signals in the string so its authority is placed first. **Case [2]:** <u>See also</u> ranks lower in Chart B, so its case is placed next. ***The second sentence*** of this passage is supported by cases [3] and [4] and uses [no signal] and <u>see generally</u>. **Case [3]:** This case directly supports the proposition. [No signal] is the highest ranked signal and is placed first in the string. **Case [4]:** <u>See generally</u> is a background-type signal and ranks lowest. An explanatory parenthetical puts the case in context; see the discussion of explanatory parentheticals in Part C of this chapter.

3. Using Short Forms with Signals

• **Basic Rule:** Short forms may be used with signals following the ordinary rules for short forms discussed in Chapter 1 of this guide. When using multiple authorities in a string citation, see discussion of short forms with strings on page 125 of this chapter.

✗ **Exception for id.:** When the immediately preceding citation contains more than one citation (i.e., a string citation), <u>id.</u> cannot be used. Instead, use the alternate short form for the specific authority.

Example:

The statutes do not refer to the license held by a professional who has yet to establish a practice. <u>O'Brien v. O'Brien</u>, 66 N.Y.2d 576, 586 (1985). Furthermore, there is no legal or logical reason to restrict the statute's plain language to existing practices. **See <u>id.</u> at 586;** <u>see e.g.</u>, <u>Arvantides v. Arvantides</u>, 64 N.Y.2d 1033, 1033 (1985). A license represents a privilege conferred upon the professional spouse and the determination that a professional license is marital property is consistent with the conceptual basis of the statute. **See <u>O'Brien</u>, 66 N.Y.2d at 586.**

C. Explanatory Parentheticals   Rules 1.5, B1.3

Explanatory parentheticals provide additional information about the authority cited without the need for a detailed discussion in the text. Explanatory parentheticals can be used to provide context for the authority or to clarify the use of a particular signal. They are most commonly used with cases, but can be used with any type of authority.

The Bluebook either encourages or strongly recommends using explanatory parentheticals with some signals to briefly explain the relationship between the authority and the proposition stated. However, explanatory parentheticals can be used with any signal if it will help the reader follow your argument. The chart below shows which signals should be accompanied by explanatory parentheticals.

Parenthetical Not Necessary (but may be helpful)	Parenthetical Encouraged	Parenthetical Strongly Recommended
[No signal] E.g., Accord See See also Contra	See also See generally	Cf. Compare But cf.

- **Basic Rule No. 1: All Citations.** Succinctly explain the relevance of the cited proposition, placing the explanation in parentheses at the end of the citation.

  - Parenthetical information should be as concise as possible without sacrificing clarity.

  - Omit articles and prepositions unless the result would be confusing.

  - Do not capitalize the first letter unless quoting an entire sentence.

  - Place citation-ending punctuation outside the closing parenthesis.

- **Basic Rule No. 2: Participial Phrases.** Explanatory phrases often begin with the present participle form of a verb (one that ends with -ing). Use the following to determine whether a participial phrase is necessary.

  - **Use a Participial Phrase When:** A *court* is taking action. Begin the parenthetical with a present participle form of a verb when describing an action taken by a court such as holding, finding, affirming, interpreting, etc.

  - **Do Not Use a Participial Phrase When:** You are stating facts, rules of law, or contextual information about a case, or the cited authority is a statute or other type of primary authority.

- **Basic Rule No. 3: Quotations.** If the explanatory parenthetical consists *entirely* of a quoted sentence, place the entire sentence in quotation marks, capitalize the first word, and place the quotation's ending punctuation *inside* the closing parenthesis. Place citation-ending punctuation after the closing parenthesis. See the examples on the next page.

  ☞ Indicate any omissions or alterations to the quoted material following rules 5.2 and 5.3.

Examples: Explanatory Parentheticals

With Present Participle	Various items may be considered dangerous weapons, but rope is not one of them. <u>Smith v. Baldwin</u>, 466 F.3d 805, 818 (9th Cir. 2006) (**finding** no evidence rope is dangerous weapon under Oregon statutes).
	An outcry by a victim is a circumstance the jury can consider on the question of corroboration. <u>Riggins v. State</u>, 226 Ga. 381, 385 (Ga. 1970) (**rejecting** defendant's argument that outcry goes only to question of consent, not to corroboration).
Without Present Participle *Facts* ☞	The corroboration of an accomplice's testimony in cases of crimes for hire may consist primarily of the defendant's statements tending to connect the defendant to the crime. <u>Ex parte Bullock</u>, 770 So. 2d 1062, 1068 (Ala. 2000) (**arson for hire**); <u>Prewitt v. State</u>, 460 So. 2d 296 (Ala. Crim. App. 1984) (**murder for hire**).
Rule of Law ☞	A primary rationale espoused in most cases invoking the Firefighters Rule centers upon assumption of risk. <u>Herman v. Welland Chem., Ltd.</u>, 580 F. Supp. 823, 831 (M.D. Pa. 1984) (**firefighters assume risk of injury while on duty**).
Info About Statute ☞	Persons who actively participate in any criminal street gang may have their sentences enhanced. Cal. Penal Code § 186.22(b)(1) (Deering 2011) (**five to ten years, depending on seriousness of underlying felony**).
Full-Sentence Quotation in Parenthetical	Determining if a waiver is valid is based on whether the university had the authority to waive Eleventh Amendment immunity. <u>In re Innes</u>, 184 F.3d 1275, 1284 (10th Cir. 1999) (**"Nothing in the statute itself makes entering into a contract waiving immunity an *ultra vires* act."**).

Signals and Explanatory Parentheticals Are Not a Substitute for Analysis!

It is easy to abuse both signals and explanatory parentheticals. While they are useful tools, writers should be wary of misuse. Do not substitute either tool for actual analysis of the cited authorities. Do not slap a signal such as "see generally" in front of a citation and convince yourself that the signal substitutes for explaining the relevant case law. Use explanatory parentheticals only for information that is simple and not an important part of your discussion or argument. If the material is important to the issue, always explain it in the text.

10 Quotations

Bluebook **Whitepages Rule 5 and Bluepages Rule B5** control the style for quotations in legal documents. This chapter discusses the following:

A. The basic form of quotations, beginning on this page;

B. Making alterations to quotations, beginning on page 137; and

C. Omitting portions of quoted material, beginning on page 139.

A. Form of Quotations   Rules 5.1, B5.1

- **Basic Rule:** Count the number of words in the quoted passage. If the quoted passage contains:

1. **Fifty words or more,** use a **block quotation,** following the rules described in Part 1, below.

2. **Forty-nine or fewer** words, use a **short quotation,** incorporating the quoted material directly into your text sentence or paragraph, following the rules described in Part 2, below.

Examples: Quotations

Block Quote 50 Words or More—Rule 5.1(a)	Shorter Quote 49 Words or Less—Rule 5.1(b)
There are just a few simple rules for dealing with a block quote: Whenever you use a quotation of fifty words or more, place the quoted text in a block quote. Block quotes are created by indenting both sides of the quoted material. When a block quote is used, **do not use quotation marks**. The block quote should be single spaced, and fully justified. Place the citation for the quotation at the left margin, being sure to skip a line between the end of the block quote and the citation. Smith v. Johnson, 555 P.2d 555 (Ore. 2010).	When your quotation is less than fifty words, you must "incorporate the quote directly into your sentence," placing the quoted material within quotation marks. Smith v. Jones, 555 P.2d 555 (Ore. 2010). When a quote is incorporated into a text sentence, commas and periods are "placed inside the ending quotation mark." Id. at 556. Always be sure to follow the quotation "with a citation, including a pinpoint cite." **Id. at 557.**

1. Block Quotations   Rule 5.1(a)

- **Basic Rule:** For quotations of fifty or more words:

  (a) Single space;

  (b) Fully justify;

  (c) Indent left and right;

  (d) **Do not** enclose in quotation marks; and

  (e) Follow with a citation to the quote's source, placed at the **left margin** of the paper (i.e., not part of the block quote itself), leaving one blank line between the end of the block quotation and the citation.

2. Short Quotations   Rule 5.1(b)

- **Basic Rule:** Shorter passages of forty-nine or fewer words are incorporated into the text of the document as follows:

  (a) Place the quoted passage in quotation marks;

  (b) Do not change the format, i.e., do not indent or change the line spacing; and

  (c) Follow the quote immediately with a citation to the quote's source.

  (d) Whether punctuation is placed inside the quotation marks depends on the type and usage of the punctuation mark.

    - **Commas and Periods:** Always place inside the closing quote mark.

    - **Semicolons:** Place outside the closing quote mark.

    - **Question Marks:** Place inside *or* outside the closing quote mark, depending on whether the question mark is part of the quote itself (place inside), or it punctuates the non-quoted material (place outside).

    - **Exclamation Points:** Place inside the closing quote mark if it is part of the quote itself.

      ☞ Exclamation points that are not part of a quote are not used in formal legal writing. Change to a period.

Examples: Punctuation

Period or Comma	• The court held the statute applied "in the absence of explicit consent."
	• Counterclaims in this situation are "compulsory," not optional.
Semicolon	• The State has an obligation to make "reasonable efforts toward reunification"; a parent has an equal obligation.
Question Mark	• Jarrod asked his co-defendant "why the gun?"
	• Should the court grant "immunity"?
Exclamation Point	• The victim screamed "get out!"
	• This Court should reverse the district court's decision because the district court judge "got it wrong"!
	☞ Do not use exclamation points in legal writing except when they are part of quoted material. Change the exclamation point in the second example to a period, and place inside the closing quote mark.

B. Alterations   Rule 5.2

Sometimes it is necessary to slightly alter a quotation so that it fits neatly into the structure of your sentence or paragraph, or to insert a word to help the reader better understand the quoted material. If an alternation is made, that alteration, no matter how small, must be made known to the reader. This is accomplished by the use of brackets around the altered material.

• **Basic Rule: All Alterations.** Enclose the altered material in brackets. To add a word or phrase, enclose the addition in brackets. To omit letters from a root word, or to change a plural to singular, use empty brackets. See examples below.

• **Basic Rule: Emphasis.** To emphasize a word or phrase in a quotation that is not emphasized in the original, convert the emphasized text to italics, then add a parenthetical at the end of the citation enclosing the words "emphasis added."

    ☞ If the word or phrase is emphasized in the original, keep that emphasis, but DO NOT add a parenthetical saying the emphasis was in original. This makes sense if you consider that you are not *altering* the text if you are copying the original emphasis.

    ☞ *Bluebook* Rule 5.2 discusses additional, less common, situations you may encounter when altering quotations, including the use of "sic" to indicate a mistake in the original, and altering quotations within quotations. Consult *The Bluebook* if you encounter these situations.

Examples: Altering Quotations

Original	Altered
"**A** final judgment on the merits of an action precludes the parties or their privies from **relitigating** issues that were or could have been raised in that action." <u>Federated Dep't Stores v. Moitie</u>, 452 U.S. 394, 398 (1981).	The United States Supreme Court has held that **"[a]** final judgment on the merits of an action precludes the parties or their privies from **_relitigating_** issues that were or could have been raised in that action." <u>Federated Dep't Stores v. Moitie</u>, 452 U.S. 394, 398 (1981) **(emphasis added)**.
	☞ The **"a"** has been changed from a capital to lower case, indicated by placing the "a" in brackets. The word **relitigating** has been emphasized by changing the typeface to italics and adding a parenthetical to the end of the citation.
"**Having** determined that **Melia** is not entitled to prevail under either theory upon which recovery was sought, we need not discuss the punitive damage issue raised by **Dillon**." <u>Melia v. Dillon Co.</u>, 18 Kan. App. 2d 5, 10 (1993).	The court concluded that, **"[h]**aving determined that **[plaintiff]** is not entitled to prevail under either theory upon which recovery was sought, we need not discuss the punitive damage issue raised by **[defendant]**." <u>Melia v. Dillon Co.</u>, 18 Kan. App. 2d 5, 10 (1993).
	☞ Three changes have been made here: (1) capitalization; (2) substituting "plaintiff" for one party's name; and (3) substituting "defendant" for the other party's name.
The death of an insured from a gunshot wound sustained while the insured, as the aggressor, was attempting to take the pistol from another, is "caused by accidental means within the double indemnity **provisions** of the policy." <u>Mohn v. Am. Cas. Co. of Reading</u>, 326 A.2d 346, 349 (Pa. 1974).	The death of an insured from a gunshot wound sustained while the insured, as the aggressor, was attempting to take the pistol from another, is "caused by accidental means within the double indemnity **provision[ ]** of the policy." <u>Mohn v. Am. Cas. Co. of Reading</u>, 326 A.2d 346, 349 (Pa. 1974).
	☞ The plural "provisions" was changed to the singular "provision." Omission of a letter is indicated by empty brackets.

☞ Do not overuse alterations because they tend to distract and slow down the reader. Instead of quoting with multiple alterations, try paraphrasing.

C. Omissions   Rule 5.3

Quotations can be shortened to omit unnecessary detail. Any omission must be clearly indicated to the reader, no matter how small.

- **Basic Rule No. 1: All Omissions.** Omission are indicated by a series of three periods, known as an ellipsis. Periods in the ellipsis must be surrounded by spaces before, between and after each period.

  ☞ *Right:*   "Include spaces . . . before, between and after each period."

  ☞ *Wrong:*   "Include spaces...before, between and after each period."

- **Basic Rule No. 2: Omitting Beginning of Quote.** To omit material at the beginning of a quote, simply add quotation marks at the start of your quote. **Do not use a leading ellipsis.**

  ☞ *Right:*   "[S]tart the quoted passage with quote marks."

  ☞ *Wrong:*   ". . . [D]o not use a leading ellipsis."

- **Basic Rule No. 3: Omitting Middle of Quote.** To omit material from the middle of a quoted passage, insert an ellipsis in place of the excised words.

  ☞ *Right:*   "Use three periods to indicate an . . . omission from the middle of a sentence."

  ☞ *Wrong:*   "Don't forget...the spaces between the periods."

- **Basic Rule No. 4: Omitting End of Quote.** To omit material at the **end** of a quote which also ends your sentence, use an ellipsis PLUS the final punctuation for your sentence (e.g. four periods, or three periods and a question mark).

  ☞ *Right:*   "Use four periods to indicate an omission at the end of a sentence . . . ."

  ☞ *Wrong:*   "Don't forget the sentence-ending punctuation . . ."

☞ Some publishers use asterisks [***] instead of periods to indicate omissions of material. This is not *Bluebook* style; use only periods to indicate omissions.

Examples: Omissions in Quotations

Location of Omitted Material	Original Quotation	Quotation with Omissions
Beginning of Quote	"~~Under federal maritime law~~, in exercising its in personam jurisdiction in maritime cases, a state may adopt such remedies as it sees fit so long as it does not make changes in the substantive law." <u>Moragne v. States Marine Lines, Inc.</u>, 398 U.S. 375, 402 (1970).	"**[I]n** exercising its in personam jurisdiction in maritime cases, a state may adopt such remedies as it sees fit so long as it does not make changes in the substantive law." <u>Moragne v. States Marine Lines, Inc.</u>, 398 U.S. 375, 402 (1970). ☞ Do not use leading ellipses. Indicate change of case with brackets.
Middle of Quote	"Under federal maritime law~~, in exercising its in personam jurisdiction in maritime cases,~~ a state may adopt such remedies as it sees fit so long as it does not make changes in the substantive law." <u>Moragne v. States Marine Lines, Inc.</u>, 398 U.S. 375, 402 (1970).	"Under federal maritime **law . . . a** state may adopt such remedies as it sees fit so long as it does not make changes in the substantive law." <u>Moragne v. States Marine Lines Inc.</u>, 398 U.S. 375, 402 (1970).
End of Quote/ End of Sentence	"Under federal maritime law, in exercising its in personam jurisdiction in maritime cases, a state may adopt such remedies as it sees fit ~~so long as it does not make changes in the substantive law~~." <u>Moragne v. States Marine Lines, Inc.</u>, 398 U.S. 375, 402 (1970).	"Under federal maritime law, in exercising its in personam jurisdiction in maritime cases, a state may adopt such remedies as it **sees fit . . . .**" <u>Moragne v. States Marine Lines, Inc.</u>, 398 U.S. 375, 402 (1970). ☞ Include final punctuation when the omitted portion of the quote ends your sentence (i.e., 4 periods, not three).

A Little Guidance on Omissions

Although *The Bluebook* provides rules for *how* to omit text from quotations, it does not provide rules for determining *how much* of the text to quote or what to omit. Here are a few tips to help you decide.

- Quote as little as possible. In most circumstances, it is unnecessary to quote an entire sentence. Instead, paraphrase the sentence and quote only the key language: the three or four words you want your reader to notice.

- If a longer quote is necessary, keep omissions to a minimum. Too many omissions in a single sentence or passage makes the reader wonder what was left out—has the meaning been accidently (or deliberately!) altered by dropping some words? It is far better to paraphrase the passage and quote only the key language.

- Rarely (as in almost never) quote a fifty-plus word passage requiring a block quotation. Rarely (as in almost never) is the language of the entire passage so vital that it cannot be paraphrased and shortened. Busy readers tend to skip or skim block quotes, potentially missing the point you are making, and rendering the entire block quote useless. With the possible exception of critical language in a statute that cannot be paraphrased without changing its meaning, avoid block quotes by using a combination of paraphrasing and short quotations of key language.

11 Capitalization

Bluebook Whitepages Rule 8 and Bluepages Rule B7.3 control the capitalization of certain words and names in textual sentences. This chapter discusses the following rules:

A. General capitalization rules, beginning on this page; and

B. Special capitalization rules for court documents and proceedings, beginning on page 145.

A. Capitalization Basics   Rules 8, B8

- **Basic Rule No. 1: Titles and Headings.** Capitalize all words in titles or headings, even if the word is not capitalized in the original.

    ✗ **Exception:** Do not capitalize articles, conjunctions or prepositions that are **less than five** letters, UNLESS it is the first word of a heading or title, or follows a colon. Rule 8(a).

    Examples:

    > **Heading:** **The** Measure Was Materially Relevant **to the** Attainment **of the** Military Purpose.
    >
    > **Title:** Seven Pillars **of a** New Evidentiary Paradigm: **The** Food, Drug, **and** Cosmetic Act Enters **the** Genomic Era.

- **Basic Rule No. 2: Specific Persons or Groups.** Capitalize nouns that identify SPECIFIC persons, officials, groups, government offices or government bodies; do not capitalize when the noun is a general reference. Rule 8(c).

    Examples:

    > The **President** spoke briefly.
    >
    > The various organizations' **presidents** met briefly.
    >
    > The **Congress** met in regular session.
    >
    > The **congressional** committees gave their reports.

- **Basic Rule No. 3: Other Words.** Certain words when used in certain contexts should always be capitalized. See *Bluebook* Rule 8(c) and the chart on the next page.

Examples: Capitalized Words   Rule 8(c)

Capitalize	Under These Circumstances	Examples
Act	When referring to a specific legislative act.	The proposed **Act** will ensure privacy. **But not:** Legislatures in several states passed similar **acts**.
Circuit	When used with a circuit's name or number.	The Eleventh **Circuit** held the opposite. **But not:** Two **circuits** held the opposite.
Code	When referring to a specific statutory code.	The Delaware **Code** bars the conduct. **But not:** The state's **code** required approval before proceeding.
Commonwealth	When it is part of the full title of a state, or when the word it modifies is capitalized, or it is a party to the litigation.	The **Commonwealth** of Kentucky. **But not:** Whether a **commonwealth** can impose this form of tax is unclear.
Constitution	When referring to the United States Constitution, or when naming any constitution in full.	The New Mexico **Constitution**. **But not:** Every state has a **constitution**.
Court	When naming any court in full, or when referring to the United States Supreme Court.	The Florida Supreme **Court** held the statute was ambiguous. **But not:** A **court** previously ruled against the plaintiff in a similar case.
Federal	When the word it modifies is capitalized.	The **Federal** Indian Health Service oversees the programs. **But not:** Whether **federal** authorities have that right is debatable.
Judge, Justice	When giving the name of a specific judge or justice, or when referring to a Justice of the Supreme Court.	**Chief Justice** John G. Roberts, Jr. **But not:** The **judge** ruled quickly.

Chart continues on the next page.

Examples: Capitalized Words, *continued*

Capitalize	Under These Circumstances	Examples
State	When it is the part of the full title of a state or if the word it modifies is capitalized.	The **State** of Iowa agreed to render aid. **But not:** Whether the **states** would agree was unclear.
Term	When referring to a term of the United States Supreme Court.	The **Term** of the Court began yesterday. **But not:** It was the beginning of the senator's **term** in office.

☞ This chart illustrates the Basic Rule only. There are additional requirements. See examples and exceptions in *Bluebook* Rule 8.

☞ Also see the rules for capitalization in court documents, discussed in the next section of this guide.

B. Court Documents and Proceedings   Rule B8

• In practitioners' documents, including office memoranda and documents that will be submitted to a court, the following words *may* need to be capitalized:

(1). The word "court";

(2) Words designating parties to a legal action;

(3) The titles of court documents; and

(4) The titles of court proceedings.

1. Courts   Rule B8

• **Basic Rule:** In text sentences, do not capitalize the word court when making a general reference to a court. Always capitalize the word "court" when referring to any of the following:

(a) The full name of a specific court;

(b) The United States Supreme Court; and

(c) The court that will be receiving the document.

☞ In other words, capitalize if you are referring to the Court that is deciding *your* matter. If you are referring to a different court, such as a court that decided a precedent case you are discussing, do not capitalize.

Examples: Capitalization of Court

Capitalization Rule	Examples
(a) Full Name of Any Court	The **Fifth Circuit Court of Appeals** held similarly.
(b) United States Supreme Court	The **Supreme Court** recently held the statute was unconstitutional.
	The Court recently held the statute was unconstitutional.
(c) Receiving Court (i.e., YOUR court)	Furthermore, **this Court** should reconsider the Plaintiff's motion.
	However, **the court** ruled in the plaintiff's favor in <u>Smith</u>.

2. Parties to a Legal Action   Rule B8

• **Basic Rule:** Capitalize any words referring to parties to *your* legal action. Do not capitalize party designations in other legal actions (e.g., parties in precedent cases).

Examples: Capitalization of Party Names

Capitalize parties to YOUR legal action. This includes designations such as: • Plaintiff and Defendant • Appellant and Appellee • Petitioner and Respondent • Movant	The **Petitioner** failed to timely file a reply to **Respondent's** opposing brief. The **Plaintiff** in our case testified that the **Defendant** was talking on his cell phone at the time of the accident.
Do not capitalize parties who are part of ANOTHER legal action, including precedent cases.	In the <u>Sheffield</u> case, the **defendant** was similarly talking on his cell phone at the time he struck the **plaintiff's** car.

3. Titles of Court Documents   Rule B8

- **Basic Rule:** Capitalize the full or shortened titles of documents prepared in connection with *your* legal action. Do not capitalize generic names of court documents filed in your case, or court documents filed in other cases (e.g., precedent cases).

Examples: Capitalization of Court Document Titles

Titles of documents in YOUR action	The Plaintiff's **Motion for Summary Judgment** should be denied.
Generic references in YOUR action	In our case, all **motions** should be heard concurrently.
Titles of documents and generic references in ANOTHER action	The plaintiff's **motion for summary judgment** was denied in <u>Tatum</u>.

4. Court Proceedings   Rule B8

- **Basic Rule:** Capitalize the full title of court proceedings in connection with your legal action. Do not capitalize generic references in your case or proceedings in other cases (e.g., precedent cases).

Examples: Capitalization of Court Proceedings

Full title of proceedings in YOUR action	Our client's **Pretrial Hearing** is scheduled for Monday, July 15.
Generic reference to proceedings in YOUR action	We request that the **hearing** be held at least one week before the **trial**.
Proceedings in ANOTHER action	In <u>Miller</u>, the court held a **pretrial hearing**, then **trial** commenced.

5. Judges   Rule B8

- **Basic Rule: Judges and Justices.** Always capitalize the title judge or justice in the following circumstances:

  (1) When giving the full name of a judge or justice;

(2) When referring to Justices of the U.S. Supreme Court and, although not required by *The Bluebook*, when referring to Justices of your state's highest court.

(3) When referring to the Judge who is hearing your matter, but not when referring to judges or justices in another matter, including precedent cases.

Examples: Capitalization of Judges and Justices

Full Name of Judge or Justice	The opinion was written by **Justice** Albert Broadhurst. The opinion was written by **Justice** Broadhurst.
Supreme Court Justices	Two **Justices** joined the dissenting opinion in the Johnson case.
Judge in YOUR matter Judge in ANOTHER matter	The **Judge** advised us that our case will be postponed. The trial court **judge** ruled the statute of limitations was tolled.

12 Numbers, Numerals, Ordinals, and Symbols

Bluebook **Whitepages** Rule 6.2 controls how numbers, numerals, and ordinals are written in documents, and provides rules for inclusion of symbols in textual sentences. This chapter discusses the following:

A. When to spell out numbers, and when to use numerals, beginning on this page;

B. Using ordinals, beginning on page 151; and

C. Using section, paragraph, and percent symbols, and dollar signs, beginning on page 151.

A. Numbers and Numerals   Rule 6.2(a)

- **Basic Rule No. 1:** Spell out the numbers zero to ninety-nine in textual sentences. Use numerals for numbers 100 and larger.

  ✗ **Exception 1:** Spell out numbers in the following situations:

  (a) Any number that begins a sentence; and

  (b) Round numbers (optional).

  ✗ **Exception 2:** <u>Use numerals</u> in the following situations:

  (a) Numbers in a series that includes numbers both greater and less than 100;

  (b) Numbers that include decimals; and

  (c) Numbers that include repeated percentages or dollar amounts.

- **Basic Rule No. 2: Commas.** For numbers four digits or larger, use commas to separate thousands. Rule 6.2(vii).

Examples: Numbers and Numerals

Rule	Applies to:	Example
Basic Rule No. 1	Numbers zero to ninety-nine	Several witnesses, including **three** eyewitnesses, testified at the trial.
Basic Rule No. 1	Numbers 100 and larger	Organizers said **175** people attended the meeting.
Exception No. 1(a)	Numbers that begin sentences	**Two hundred twenty** people attended the rally.
Exception No. 1(b)	Round numbers	A **thousand** replies were received.
Exception No. 2(a)	Numbers in a series	The police detained, arrested, and interviewed **55**, **17**, and **135** persons, respectively.
Exception No. 2(a)	Numbers *not* in a series	In total, there were **fifty-five** detained for questioning that day, **seventeen** were arrested, and police interviewed at least **135** witnesses at the scene.
Exception No. 2(b)	Decimals	The plaintiff's temperature was **99.5** before she was given medication.
Exception No. 2(c)	Multiple percentages and dollar amounts	The fee will be discounted **25%** if payment is received within **ten** days, **20%** if payment is received within **twenty** days, and **10%** for payment within **thirty** days. Thus, if payment is made within **ten** days, deduct **$25**, within **twenty** days, deduct **$20**, and within **thirty** days, deduct **$10**.
Basic Rule No. 2	Numbers with four or more digits	3,966 55,324

B. Ordinals   Rule 6.2(b)

- **Basic Rule No. 1: Text Sentences.** When a numeral is followed by an ordinal, use a two-letter abbreviation for the ordinal [101**st**, 102**nd**, 103**rd**, etc.].

  ☞ 102**nd** anniversary of the landmark decision.

  ☞ Do not use superscript.

  Right: 102**nd**

  Wrong: 102**nd**

- **Basic Rule No. 2: Citations.** Basic Rule No. 1, above, applies only to ordinals in text sentences, NOT citations. In citations, use "2d" and "3d" when referring to a second or third series number or judicial division. Use two-letter abbreviations for all other series or divisions.

  Examples:

  ☞ Use One-Letter Abbreviations: N.E.2**d**   3**d** Cir.

  ☞ Use Two-Letter Abbreviations: 1**st** Cir.   4**th** Dist.   A.L.R.5**th**

C. Symbols   Rules 6.2(c)–(d)

- **Basic Rule No. 1: Section and Paragraph Symbols.** Spell out the words "section" and "paragraph" in text sentences, except when referring to sections of the United States Code. In citation sentences, use section (§ or §) or paragraph (¶) symbols. **Insert one space** between the symbol and the numeral.

  ☞ See "How to Create Section and Paragraph Symbols" at the end of this chapter.

- **Basic Rule No. 2: Dollar Signs and Percent Symbols.** Spell out the words "dollar" and "percent" whenever numbers are spelled out. Use the symbols for dollars ($) and percentage (%) whenever numerals are used. DO NOT insert a space between the symbol and the numeral.

  ☞ See discussion of when to spell out numbers in Part A of this chapter.

Examples: Symbols

Section in text sentence	The issue was addressed in **section 122** of the document.
Paragraph in text sentence	The issue was addressed in **paragraph 122** of the document.
Section in citation sentence	The act was a crime. **§ 15.3.14.**
Paragraph in citation sentence	The witness testified to the event. (Doe Aff. **¶ 24.**)
Dollars with spelled-out number	The price was **ten dollars**.
Dollars with numerals	The price was **$250**.
Percent with spelled-out number	The passage rate for the exam was **seventy-five percent**.
Percent with numerals	The price rose **150%**.
Beginning of a sentence	**One hundred fifty percent** price increases were common.

How to Create Symbols

To create section (§ or §) or paragraph (¶) symbols in Word, follow these instructions.

PC: From the "insert" drop down menu, select "symbol." Look through the collection of symbols for the § or ¶ symbol. Double-click on the symbol to insert.

SHORTCUT: Hold down the ALT key and type 21 for a section symbol, or 20 for a paragraph symbol on the numeric keypad. The symbol will appear when you release the ALT key.

NOTE: This shortcut will work only if you enter the number using the numeric keypad located on the right side of the keyboard. The PC shortcut will not work by using the number keys at the top of the keyboard. On laptops that do not have a numeric keypad, the shortcuts will only work if the "NumLk" is toggled to convert the right hand keys into a numeric keypad.

Mac: Hold down the OPTION key and type 6 for a section symbol, or 7 for a paragraph symbol. This works the same on both desktop and laptop models.

13 Electronic Sources

Bluebook **Whitepages Rule 18 and Bluepages Rule B18** control citations to electronic sources. Additional rules apply to specific types of sources.

When the first edition of the *Bluebook* was released in 1926, there was no such thing as an electronic database, and citations to cases, statutes, and other legal materials could only be made to their printed form—nothing else existed. Of course things have changed. While law libraries and lawyers' offices are still crammed with print sets of case reports, codes, and secondary authorities, practitioners increasingly turn to electronic sources for their day-to-day research needs.

Even after the switch to electronic sources, *The Bluebook* continues to strongly encourage citation to print versions of legal materials. As a general rule, electronic versions of authorities are to be cited only if the material is not readily available in print. Of course "readily available" is open to interpretation, and most practitioners routinely cite to electronic versions they obtained from "reliable sources."

Although the content is the same whether you are using print or electronic versions, the form for the citation may differ. For example, a statute photocopied from a printed code set will say exactly the same thing as a statute from an online legal database, but the citation must be adjusted to indicate whether your *source* was a print or electronic version.

This Chapter discusses citations to the two largest commercial databases, Westlaw and LEXIS, citations to Internet authorities for some authorities, and offers an optional, non-*Bluebook*-approved alternate form for practitioners to replace some of the more cumbersome *Bluebook* forms. The following authorities are included:

A. Cases, beginning on page 155;

B. Statutory law, beginning on page 160;

C. Constitutions, beginning on page 163;

D. Regulations, beginning on page 164;

E. Procedural and court rules, beginning on page 165; and

F. Secondary sources, beginning on page 166.

A Note About Reliable Sources

The Bluebook allows citations to "reliable" online sources — ones that have long track records of trustworthiness. Here is some guidance for choosing reliable sources.

Commercial Databases: Reliable. The large commercial databases, including Westlaw, LEXIS, Bloomberg, VersusLaw, and Loislaw, are all reliable sources and can be cited directly.

Court and Government Websites: Reliable, With Caution. Sites maintained by a governmental body are reliable if the document is "authenticated" or is an "official version" as described below.

Internet Websites (Non-Governmental): Not Reliable for Primary Authority. Although information found on many websites may be accurate, sites maintained by individuals or organizations should not be cited for primary authority as they lack the history of reliability of the commercial databases. They may be cited for some secondary sources when the information is not available from another, reliable, source, as discussed in this Chapter.

Authenticated Documents: Available for most federal government documents and many state documents, these are encrypted to prevent tampering. An authenticated document will have a certificate, logo, or digital signature attesting to its authenticity. Look for an indication of authenticity on the document itself, or elsewhere on the website.

Official Versions: Many states designate an "official source" for documents, usually maintained on the state's official website. Look for words indicating the document (or website) is official.

A Note About Practitioners' Alternate Forms (Optional)

The Bluebook forms for citation to electronic sources do not necessarily reflect the needs of practitioners. Those forms often include redundant information, or information in a form that is not useful in practice. Additionally, a practitioners' cite to one commercial database is not useful if the reader only has access to a different database. Local customs generally translate the *Bluebook's* forms into something more practical for use in law offices.

This guide offers an alternate form for citations to most of the sources discussed in this section. These alternate forms are NOT in *Bluebook* form, rather they show another way to cite the source that is tailored to practitioners' needs. It is more consistent in form between different sources, while still providing all information required for easy location of the source material in any commercial database.

☞ **Before using a practitioners' alternate form, be sure to check with your instructor or supervisor. While you are learning citation, you may be asked to follow *Bluebook* form.**

A. Cases   Rules 18.3, 10.8, B10.1.4

Any case printed in a hardbound print volume is also available from electronic sources. In addition, many "unreported" cases, also known as "unpublished" cases, are available electronically. Citation forms vary between published and unpublished opinions, as explained below. This Part discusses the following topics:

1. Citing published decisions to commercial databases, beginning on page 156;

2. Citing unpublished decisions to commercial databases, beginning on page 157; and

3. Citing Authenticated or Official decisions from a government website on page 160.

About Unpublished Decisions

In response to the growing number of cases winding through the appellate process, more and more decisions are designated as **"unpublished opinions."** These are decisions that the court determines are of insufficient precedential value to warrant publication in official reporters. Often these cases are cumulative, applying well-established rules of law to facts similar to those in prior cases. Although not appearing in print reporters (except the Federal Appendix, discussed later in this chapter), they are widely available through commercial databases and court websites.

When to cite unpublished opinions—if at all—is beyond the scope of this guide, but it is important to learn to identify unpublished opinions that you will come across when researching in commercial databases. The following are clues that you might be looking at an unpublished opinion.

1. Look for a notation at the top of the opinion stating "not for publication" or "not released for publication," or similar phrases.

2. For cases retrieved from a commercial database, look for a citation to the hardbound print reporters. If the only available citation is to the database, you probably have an unpublished opinion. However, if the case is very recent, it may not have been assigned a citation in the print reporters, or the citation may include blank lines: ___ N.W.2d ___. For very recent cases, you may not be able to tell if the case will be published; see the next clue.

3. If you have a recent case, be sure to check local rules to determine the jurisdiction's practice with respect to the finality of decisions. In some jurisdictions, cases do not become "final" for a period of time (usually 30 days) after the decision is released. Other jurisdictions may publish a case that was previously labeled unpublished, or may withdraw a case from publication (de-publish). Always verify the current status of recent decisions before citing.

1. Commercial Databases: Published Decisions   Rules 18.3, 10.8, B10.1.4

Citations to published cases are exactly the same, whether you are using a copy of the case from the print reporter or a version downloaded from an electronic database. All of the information necessary to cite the case appears on the electronic version. However, an extra step may be required to determine the pinpoint page number, as discussed below.

- **Basic Rule: Full Citation:** Follow the rules discussed in Chapter 2 of this guide for the basic citation form. If the commercial database uses a system of "star paging" to provide the pinpoint, see the discussion below.

- **Basic Rule: Short Form:** Follow the rules for short form citations discussed in Chapter 2 of this Guide.

☞ As commercial databases evolve, you may find that the "stars" have been replaced by an ordinary page numbers—sans stars, or you may be able to hover over the passage until a pop-up window appears with citation information. In these situations, use the page numbers provided.

Determining Pinpoints Using Star Paging

It is a contradiction in terms to base a claim for intentional infliction of emotional distress on mere "negligent misinformation."

You are writing a memo that will include the above passage from the <u>Fitzgerald</u> case found in Appendix A to this guide. Your copy of the case was retrieved from a commercial database.

Steps For Determining Pinpoint Page Numbers

1. Locate the print reporter's citations in the case caption. Some cases are reported in only one reporter, others may be reported in two or more. Whenever there are cites to multiple reporters, they are referred to as **parallel citations**.

2. In the <u>Fitzgerald</u> caption, there are parallel citations to two reporters. The first citation is to volume 184 of the Georgia Appeals Reports, beginning on page 567; the second is to volume 362 the South Eastern Reporter, second series, beginning on page 103.

3. Draw a single asterisk (star) above the first parallel citation; draw two asterisks (stars) above the second parallel citation. If the case has additional parallel citations, mark each with the appropriate number of asterisks.

*   **

☞ **184 Ga. App. 567, 362 S.E.2d 103**

4. Determine which reporter is the "correct" reporter to cite by looking in *Bluebook* Table 1.3. Make a note of the number of asterisks assigned to the "correct" reporter. See discussion of "correct" reporters on page 34 of this guide.

Chart continues on next page

☞ You have assigned two asterisks to the South Eastern Reporter, the "correct" reporter for Georgia according to Table 1.3.

5. Next, locate the passage you wish to cite in the text of the case.

☞ In this example, the passage is shown in bold on the second page of the case.

6. To identify the page where this passage appears in the print reporter version, move **backward** in the case until you find the last page number with two asterisks. This is the print reporter page number you will use for your pinpoint cite.

☞ The passage you wish to cite can be found on page 105 of volume 362 of the South Eastern Reporter. A full citation to the passage with a pinpoint cite is:

Fitzgerald v. Caplan, 362 S.E.2d, 103, 105 (Ga. Ct. App. 1987).

Caution

It is easy to accidentally pinpoint to the wrong page number by using the *nearest* starred page number rather than the page number for the *correct reporter*. In the Fitzgerald example, above, *568 is the nearest page number for the passage you are citing, but that is the page number for the Georgia Appeals Reports (the "wrong" reporter). To avoid this problem, always double check your pinpoint page numbers for logic. If the beginning page for the case in the South Eastern Reporter is page 103, a pinpoint cite to page 568 is not logical.

2. Commercial Databases: Unpublished Decisions   Rules 10.8.1, 18.3.1

Unpublished cases are available through commercial databases but do not appear in print reporters (with a few exceptions including the Federal Appendix, discussed below). To cite unpublished cases to a commercial database, follow these rules:

- **Basic Rule: Full Citation:** Include the following information in a full citation:
  (1) Case name;
  (2) The court's docket number;
  (3) The database identifier (document number);
  (4) A pinpoint cite, preceded by the word "at" and an asterisk (star);
  (5) The identity of the jurisdiction and court issuing the decision (if necessary); and
  (6) The date, including the month, day and year of the decision.

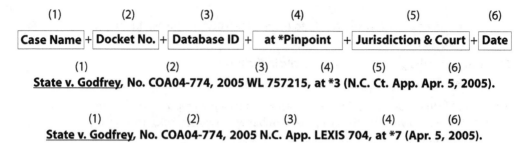

Although a citation to an unpublished case looks very different from a citation to a print reporter, it contains the same four required pieces of information: Case name, source, jurisdiction/court, and date. Use the following information, numbered to correspond to the illustration above, to adapt the standard citation form for an unpublished decision.

☞ Information is provided in this guide for citations to the two commercial databases most frequently used by practitioners: Westlaw and LEXIS. To cite to other commercial databases, follow the rules and examples in *Bluebook* Rule 10.8.1.

(1) Case Name: Prepare the same as reported cases, following the rules discussed in Chapter 2 of this guide.

(2) Docket Number: Also known as the case number, this number is assigned by the court and is used to track the case through the court system. The docket number appears in the case caption, usually below the party names.

☞ You may omit (a) an initial digit preceding a colon, or (b) a judge's initials at the end of the docket number. Before deleting the judge's initials, make sure that those initials refer to a judge, not a court. For example, SCT likely refers to a supreme court, not a judge. Approach this option with caution as it is easy to make a mistake.

(3) Database Identifier: This is a unique identification number assigned by the commercial database publisher. It is equivalent to the source information for citations to published cases in print reporters, and consists of three parts:

(a) Year (roughly equivalent to the volume number);

(b) Database name (equivalent to the reporter name), written as LEXIS, or WL (for Westlaw); and

(c) Document number (roughly equivalent to the beginning page number).

(4) Pinpoint: As with print reporters, this identifies the precise page where the cited material is found. It contains two parts:

(a) The word "at," separated from the document number by a comma; and

(b) An asterisk (star) followed by the pinpoint page number. Note that every unpublished case begins with page 1.

☞ To cite *consecutive* pages, omit the star in the ending page number: *259–60, *not* *259– *60.

(5) Jurisdiction and Court: Follow the rules for published cases described in Chapter 2 of this guide. If the database identifier clearly conveys the name of the jurisdiction or court, omit the information from the parenthetical per *Bluebook* Rule 10.4.

☞ Westlaw database identifiers do not identify either jurisdiction or court, while LEXIS does for state court cases only. Compare the Westlaw and LEXIS examples for the Godfrey case at the beginning of this section.

(6) Date: Include the month, day, and year the decision was issued. Abbreviate months according to *Bluebook* Table 12.

Examples: Full Citations to Unpublished Opinions

LEXIS	State v. Gonzalez, No.1 CA-CR 07-0923, 2009 Ariz. App. LEXIS 688, at *10–11 (Apr. 28, 2009).
	Aguayo v. Wachovia, No. C 10-01178 JSW, 2010 U.S. Dist. LEXIS 37822, at *9 (N.D. Cal. Mar. 24, 2010).
Westlaw	Lebby v. New Britain Senior High, No. HHBCV085007402, 2010 WL 654493, at *2 (Conn. Super. Ct. Jan. 20, 2010).
	Donato v. McCarthy, No. Civ. 00-39-M, 2001 WL 821532, at *3 (D.N.H. July 17, 2001).

☞ **Beware the copy and paste trap. If you copy and paste some or all of the citation information into your document, be sure to correct the form, including spacing and abbreviations.**

- **Basic Rule: Short Forms:** Follow the rules for short form citations discussed in Chapter 2 of this guide, with the following modifications:

  a. **Id. Short Form:** Include an asterisk before the pinpoint page number, if any.

  > ***Examples***:   Id.   Id. at *8.

  b. **Alternate short form:** Prepare the same way as published cases, but substitute the document identifier (year, database name, document number) for the print reporter's source information. Separate the pinpoint from the document number with a comma, then include "at," an asterisk, and the page number.

  > ***Examples***:
  > **Westlaw:**   Godfrey, 2005 WL 757215, at *8.
  > **LEXIS:**   Godfrey, 2005 N.C. App. LEXIS 704, at *8.

The Federal Appendix

Some Federal appellate court decisions that have been not been selected for official publication are nevertheless reported in a print reporter, the Federal Appendix, and are assigned citations in the same manner as any reported decision. To cite a case reported in the Federal Appendix, follow the rules for published decisions in Chapter 2 of this chapter. The Table 1.1 entry for the Federal Appendix is found in the Courts of Appeals entry.

Example: Tillman v. New Line Cinema Corp., 295 F. App'x 840, 842 (7th Cir. 2008).

---

3. Authenticated or Official Decisions   Rule 18.2.1

A growing number of courts make decisions available on their websites. Cite to a commercial database if the decision is published there. If the case is only available on the court's website, follow Rule 18.2.1, appending the URL to the end of the citation.

B. Statutes   Rules 12.5, 18.3, B12.1

Any statute printed in a hardbound print volume is also available from electronic sources. This Part discusses the following topics:

1. Citing to commercial databases, below;

2. Citing Authenticated or Official versions from a government website, beginning on page 161;

3. Short forms, beginning on page 161; and

4. Practitioners' alternate form (optional), beginning on page 162.

1. Commercial Databases   Rule 12.5, 18.2

- **Basic Rule:** Follow the rules discussed in Chapter 3 of this guide, modifying the parenthetical information as follows:

  (a) Include the name of the database in the date parenthetical. If citing an unofficial version, place the database name after the publisher's name.

(b) Include the "currency date" instead of the year the code was published.

☞ For **state** statutes, currency information will usually identify the last legislative session. See examples below and in *Bluebook* Rule 12.5.

☞ For **federal** statutes, this information will usually identify the latest public law number. If there are exceptions, include those exceptions in a separate parenthetical. See examples below and in Rule 12.5.

☞ Currency information appears either at the top or bottom of the database version of the statute.

Examples: Statutory Citations to Commercial Databases

State Official Code	Minn. Stat. § 60B.05 (LEXIS through 2019 Reg. Sess.)
	Me. Rev. Stat. tit. 12, § 8002 (Westlaw through 2020 Spec. Sess.).
State Unofficial Code	Mass. Ann. Laws ch. 19, § 6 (LexisNexis, LEXIS through 2019 Legis. Sess.)
	Utah Code Ann. § 31A-8-402.5 (West, Westlaw through 2019 Reg. Sess.).
Federal Official Code	6 U.S.C. § 746 (LEXIS through Pub. L. No. 116–17).
Federal Unofficial Code	11 U.S.C.S. § 553(b)(1)(B) (LexisNexis, LEXIS through Pub. L. No. 116-22 (excluding Pub. L. No. 116-8, 116-12, and 116-15)).
	11 U.S.C.A. § 553(b)(1)(B) (West, Westlaw through Pub. L. No. 116-22 (excluding Pub. L. No. 116-8, 116-12, and 116-15)).

2. Authenticated or Official Versions   Rule 18.2.1

• **Basic Rule:** If the document has been retrieved from an authenticated source or is an official version from a state website, cite the document as though you are citing a print copy, following the rules in Chapter 3 of this guide, and using the current year as the code year.

3. Short Forms   Rules 12.10(d), 18.8

• **Basic Rule:** Follow the rules for short form citations discussed in Chapter 3 of this guide. For citations to commercial databases, add the name of the database in a parenthetical at the end of the citation. For citations to authenticated or official versions, no additional information is needed.

   Examples:

   Id.   § 60B.05 (LEXIS).   § 60B.05 (Westlaw).

4. Practitioners' Alternate Form (Optional)

The *Bluebook* form for statutes cited to electronic databases is long, cumbersome, and does not suit the needs of practitioners. Many practitioners prefer a more practical solution that conveys the necessary information without unnecessary detail. There is no one shortcut used by all, but the following are suggestions for alternate forms.

☞ Before using an alternate form, check with your instructor or supervisor.

Option A: **Omit Redundant Publisher Name.** The two most-used databases, Westlaw and LEXIS, are owned by West and LexisNexis, respectively. When citing an unofficial code from these sources, it should be sufficient to include only the name of the database.

Option B: **Substitute Date for Currency Information.** For practitioners, there is rarely, if ever, a need to include the currency information; the date the statute was retrieved from the database is more useful. The date should be expressed as the month, day, and year. Abbreviate months according to Table 12.

　　　　☞ Commercial databases update daily, meaning the statute you cite today may be revised or repealed, and replaced in the database tomorrow. For that reason, use the full date when citing commercial databases so that, if necessary, the material can be traced back to a specific day.

Option C: **Combined Form.** Omit the publisher (Option A), and use a full date (Option B) for the shortest citation that includes all necessary information.

Short Form: Omit the parenthetical name of the database at the end of the citation.

Examples: Practitioners' Alternate Form (Optional)

Bluebook Form	Mass. Ann. Laws ch. 19, § 6 (LexisNexis, LEXIS through 2020 Legis. Sess.).
	Utah Code Ann. § 31A-8-402.5 (West, Westlaw through 2020 Reg. Sess.).
	11 U.S.C.S. § 553(b)(1)(B) (LexisNexis, LEXIS through Pub. L. No. 116-22 (excluding Pub. L. No. 116-8, 116-12, and 116-15)).
	Id. § 553(c) (Westlaw). *or* § 553(c) (Westlaw).
Option A (Publisher Omitted)	Mass. Ann. Laws ch. 19, § 6 (LEXIS through 2020 Legis. Sess.).
	Utah Code Ann. § 31A-8-402.5 (Westlaw through 2020 Reg. Sess.).
	11 U.S.C.S. § 553(b)(1)(B) (LEXIS through Pub. L. No. 116-22 (excluding Pub. L. No. 116-8, 116-12, and 116-15)).
	Id. § 553(c). *or* § 553(c).

Chart continues on the next page.

Examples: Practitioners' Alternate Form (Optional), *continued*

Option B (Substitute Date)	Mass. Ann. Laws ch. 19, § 6 (LexisNexis, LEXIS July 1, 2020). Utah Code Ann. § 31A-8-402.5 (West, Westlaw July 1, 2020). 11 U.S.C.S. § 553(b)(1)(B) (LexisNexis, LEXIS July 1, 2020). Id. § 553(c). *or* § 553(c).
Option C (Combined A & B)	Mass. Ann. Laws ch. 19, § 6 (LEXIS July 1, 2020). Utah Code Ann. § 31A-8-402.5 (Westlaw July 1, 2020). 11 U.S.C.S. § 553(b)(1)(B) (LEXIS July 1, 2020). Id. § 553(c). *or* § 553(c).

C. Constitutions   Rule 11

- **Basic Rule: Commercial Database.** Follow the rules discussed in Chapter 4 of this guide, but add a parenthetical at the end of the citation that includes the following information:

  (1) The names of the publisher and database; and

  (2) The "currentness of the database" as provided by the database. This information may be expressed as a month, day, and year; month and year; or may resemble the currency date for statutes, depending on the database you are using.

- **Basic Rule: Authenticated or Official Versions.** If the document is from an authenticated source or is an official version from a state website, cite the document as though you are citing a print copy, following the rules in Chapter 4 of this guide.

- **Basic Rule: Short Forms.** Follow the rules for constitutional short forms found in Chapter 4 of this guide.

- ✗ **Practitioners' Alternate Form (Optional):** There is little practical need to include the parenthetical information for constitutions cited to commercial databases. Many practitioners omit the parenthetical altogether, or include only the database name and full date in a parenthetical.

Examples: Constitutions

Commercial Database	U.S. Const. amend. VI (West, Westlaw through July 2020 amendments).
	Mont. Const. art. II, § 17 (LexisNexis, LEXIS through July 2020 amendments).
Authenticated or Official Version	U.S. Const. amend. VI.

Chart continues on the next page.

Examples: Constitutions, *continued*

Practitioners' Alternate Form (Commercial Databases)	U.S. Const. amend. VI.
	U.S. Const. amend. VI (Westlaw July 1, 2020).
	Mont. Const. art. II, § 17 (LEXIS July 1, 2020).
Short Forms	U.S. Const. amend. VI (Westlaw).
	Mont. Const. art. II, § 17 (LEXIS).

D. Regulations   Rules 14.4, 18.2, 18.8

Federal and state regulations are available from commercial databases and websites providing authenticated or official versions of the regulation. The citations differ depending upon which source is cited.

- **Basic Rule: Commercial Databases.** Follow the rules discussed in Chapter 5 of this guide with the following modification: Include the database identifier, separated from the date parenthetical by a comma. Do not place in parentheses.

- **Basic Rule: Authenticated or Official Versions.** If the document has been retrieved from an authenticated source or is an official version from a state website, cite the document as though you are citing a print copy. Follow the rules in Chapter 5 of this guide and Rule 18.2.1(a).

- **Basic Rule: Short Forms:** Follow the rules for short form citations discussed in Chapter 5 of this guide. For citations to authenticated or official versions, no additional information is needed. For citations to commercial databases, add the name of the database in a parenthetical at the end of the citation.

- ✗ **Practitioners' Alternate Form (Optional):** There is little practical need to include the database information for regulations cited to commercial databases when the database identifier simply repeats the regulation number. Many practitioners modify the form to include the name of the database and date it was retrieved from the database, dropping the parenthetical date in the middle. The database name may be eliminated from the short form.

Examples: Regulations

Commercial Database	15 C.F.R. § 107(b) (2020), LEXIS 15 CFR § 107.
	6 C.F.R. § 5.28 (2020), WL 6 CFR § 5.28.
	203 Ind. Admin. Code 1-1-3 (2020), LEXIS 203 IAC § 1-1-3.

Chart continues on next page

Examples: Regulations, *continued*

Authenticated or Official Version	15 C.F.R. § 107(b) (2020).
	6 C.F.R. § 5.28 (2020).
	203 Ind. Admin. Code 1-1-3 (2020).
Short Forms	Commercial Database: § 107(b) (Westlaw).
	Authenticated Version: § 107(b).
Practitioners' Alternate Form	15 C.F.R. § 107(b) (LEXIS July 1, 2020).
	6 C.F.R. § 5.28 (Westlaw July 1, 2020).
	203 Ind. Admin. Code 1-1-3 (LEXIS July 1, 2020).
	§ 107(b).

E. Procedural and Court Rules   Rule 12.9.3

- **Basic Rule: Commercial Databases.** *The Bluebook* does not provide a form for citing procedural or court rules to commercial databases. Although rules are a type of statute, using a statutory citation form with its currency date may not make sense, or require information that is not available. It is suggested that the alternate practitioners' form be used instead.

- **Basic Rule: Authenticated or Official Versions.** If the document has been retrieved from an authenticated source or is an official version from a state website, cite the document as though you are citing a print copy following the rules in Chapter 6 of this guide.

- **Basic Rule: Short Forms.** Follow the rules for short form citation discussed in Chapter 6 of this guide. For citations to authenticated or official versions, no additional information is needed. For citations to commercial databases, add the name of the database in a parenthetical at the end of the citation.

- ✘ **Practitioners' Alternate Form (Optional).** Include the name of the database and the full date the rule was retrieved from the database, placed in parentheses at the end of the citation. In short forms, omit the database parenthetical.

Examples: Procedural and Court Rules

Commercial Database	No *Bluebook* form provided.
Authenticated or Official Version	Fed. R. Crim. P. 28.
	Kan. Sup. Ct. R. 105.
Short Forms	R. 28 (Westlaw).
	R. 105 (LEXIS).

Chart continues on the next page.

Examples: Procedural and Court Rules, *continued*

Practitioners' Alternate Form (Commercial Databases)	Fed. R. Crim. P. 28 (Westlaw July 1, 2015).
	Kan. Sup. Ct. R. 105 (LEXIS July 1, 2015).
	<u>Id.</u> *or* R. 105.

F. Secondary Sources

Most secondary sources are only available in print or from commercial databases. There are unlikely any authenticated or official versions, although if one exists, it may be cited the same as a print source. If a reliable Internet source is available, it is noted below. This Part discusses the following secondary sources:

1. Treatises and books, below;

2. Periodicals, page 167;

3. Restatements, page 168;

4. Dictionaries, page 168;

5. A.L.R. Annotations, page 169; and

6. Encyclopedias, page 170.

A Note About Evolving Commercial Databases

The major commercial publishers have been going through an evolutionary process during the last few years that will continue into the foreseeable future. During this process, how information is accessed is changing. In some situations, the "old" ways of citing to file names or libraries may give way to individual file numbers, or no number at all. You may need to adapt some of the forms shown in this section to reflect how the information is currently provided by the source.

---

1. Treatises and Books   Rules 15.9, 18.2.2, 18.3

- **Basic Rule: Commercial Database.** To cite a treatise or book to a commercial database, prepare the citation according to the rules in Chapter 7 of this guide. To indicate the database source, add a comma at the end of the citation followed by the database name and the library or file name, or unique document identifier number or code; do not place in parentheses.

- **Basic Rule: Internet.** Cite to Internet sources only if the title is not published in print form or is not available from a commercial database. The citation form may vary depending on the publication. Follow rules 15.9(b) and 18.2.2.

- **Basic Rule: Ebooks.** Cite ebooks only if the title is not published in print form. To cite an ebook, follow rule 15.9(b).

- **Basic Rule: Short Forms.** Cite in the same manner as print versions discussed in Chapter 7 of this guide.

- ✘ Practitioners' Alternate Form (Optional). Most books cannot be retrieved from databases as easily as primary sources, thus the *Bluebook* form should be used with a library name or document identifier.

Examples: Treatises & Books

Commercial Database	Roger M. Milgrim, <u>Milgrim on Licensing</u> § 707 (2014), LEXIS-LICENS.
Short Form	<u>Id.</u> § 708. *or* Milgrim, <u>supra</u>, § 708.
Practitioners' Alternate Form (Optional)	Use *Bluebook* form.

2. Periodicals   Rules 16.8, 18.3

- **Basic Rule: Commercial Databases.** Follow the rules for periodicals discussed in Chapter 7 of this guide. Add the unique database identifier or code to the document following the date parenthetical, separated from the main citation with a comma; do not place in parentheses.

- **Basic Rule: Internet.** Cite to an Internet source only if the title is not published in print form or is not available from a commercial database. To cite an Internet source, see Rule 16.8(b).

- **Basic Rule: Short Forms.** Cite in the same manner as print versions discussed in Chapter 7 of this guide.

- ✘ Practitioners' Alternate Form (Optional). Include the database name in the date parenthetical if the document can be retrieved by typing in its citation (volume, publication, page number). Include the full date the document was retrieved from the database.

    ☞ If typing in the citation does not retrieve the document, follow the *Bluebook* form.

Examples: Periodicals

Commercial Database	Karen Bradshaw Schulz, <u>Information Flooding</u>, 48 Ind. L. Rev. 755, 774 (2015), 2015 WL 2912614.
Short Forms	<u>Id.</u> at 775. *or* Schulz, <u>supra</u>, at 775.
Practitioners' Alternate Form (Optional)	Karen Bradshaw Schulz, <u>Information Flooding</u>, 48 Ind. L. Rev. 755, 774 (Westlaw 2020).

3. Restatements   Rule 12.9.4

- **Basic Rule: Commercial Databases.** *The Bluebook* does not provide a form to cite Restatements to a commercial database. To create a citation, modify the rules for Restatements discussed in Chapter 7 of this guide, and follow the rules for statutory citations discussed in Part B.1 of this chapter. Include the name of the database in the date parenthetical. Use the month, day, and year the material was retrieved from the database.

- **Basic Rule: Internet.** Restatements are not available from reliable Internet sources. Cite to a print or database version.

- **Basic Rule: Short Forms.** Cite in the same manner as print versions discussed in Chapter 7 of this guide.

Examples: Restatements

Commercial Database	Restatement (Second) Conflict of L. § 273 cmt. b (Am. L. Inst. 1988) (LEXIS July 1, 2020).
Short Forms	<u>Id.</u> § 273. *or* Conflict § 273.

4. Dictionaries   Rule 15.8

- **Basic Rule: Commercial Databases.** Follow the rules for citing dictionaries discussed in Chapter 7 of this guide. Add the name of the database and the month and day the database was last updated.

- **Basic Rule: Internet.** With the ready availability of dictionaries in print and from commercial databases, there should be no need to cite a *legal* dictionary to an Internet source. To cite non-legal dictionaries to an online source, see *Bluebook* rule 15.9(b).

- **Basic Rule: Short Forms.** Cite in the same manner as print versions discussed in Chapter 7 of this guide.

- ✗ Practitioners' Alternate Form: Add an additional parenthetical with the name of the database and the date the document was retrieved from the database.

Examples: Dictionaries

Commercial Database	*Unjust Enrichment*, Ballentine's Law Dictionary (3d ed. 1969), LEXIS (database updated July 1, 2020).
	Exemplified Copy, Black's Law Dictionary (11th ed. 2019), Westlaw (database updated July 1, 2020).
Short Forms	Id. *or* Black's, supra.
Practitioners' Alternate Form (Optional)	*Unjust Enrichment*, Ballentine's Law Dictionary (3d ed. 1969) (LEXIS July 1, 2020).
	Exemplified Copy, Black's Law Dictionary (11th ed. 2019) (Westlaw July 1, 2020).

5. A.L.R. Annotations   Rule 16.8

- **Basic Rule:** Follow the rules discussed in Chapter 7 of this guide. Add the unique database identifier or code to the document following the date parenthetical, separated from the main citation with a comma.

  - ☞ Electronic versions of A.L.R.s divide the annotation into **sections** and corresponding printed page numbers may not be available. To pinpoint a specific section, follow the Basic Rule for all citations, above, citing the beginning page number for the annotation, but using the section number for the pinpoint. See example below.

- **Basic Rule: Internet.** A.L.R. annotations are not available from reliable Internet sources. Cite to a print or commercial database version.

- **Basic Rule: Short Forms.** Cite in the same manner as print versions discussed in Chapter 7 of this guide.

- ✗ Practitioners' Alternate Form (Optional). Include the name of the database in the date parenthetical and include the full date the document was retrieved from the database.

Examples: A.L.R. Annotations

Commercial Database	F. Kletter, Annotation, <u>Construction and Application of Uniform Mandatory Disposition of Detainers Act</u>, 37 A.L.R. 6th 357, § 52 (2008), 2008 WL 2496732.
Short Forms	<u>Id.</u> § 53. *or* Kletter, <u>supra</u>, § 53.
Practitioners' Alternate Form (Optional)	F. Kletter, Annotation, <u>Construction and Application of Uniform Mandatory Disposition of Detainers Act</u>, 37 A.L.R. 6th 357, § 52 (Westlaw July 1, 2020).

6. Encyclopedias   Rule 15.9

- **Basic Rule: Commercial Databases.** Follow the rules for citing encyclopedias discussed in Chapter 7 of this guide. Include the name of the database, separated from the main citation with a comma, followed by a parenthetical that states "database updated [month and year]." See example below.

- **Basic Rule: Internet.** Most encyclopedias are not available from reliable Internet sources. If you believe the source is reliable, cite according to Rule 18.2.2.

- **Basic Rule: Short Forms.** Cite in the same manner as print versions discussed in Chapter 7 of this guide.

- ✗ **Practitioner's Alternate Form.** Replace the date parenthetical with a parenthetical including the name of the database and the full date the document was retrieved from the database.

Examples: Encyclopedias

Commercial Database	2 C.J.S. <u>Adjoining Landowners</u> § 58, Westlaw (database updated July 2020).
Short Forms	<u>Id.</u> § 59. *or* C.J.S., <u>supra</u>, § 59.
Practitioners' Alternate Form (Optional)	2 C.J.S. <u>Adjoining Landowners</u> § 58 (Westlaw July 1, 2020).

Appendix: Citing Cases from Commercial Databases

Court of Appeals of Georgia.

FITZGERALD

v.

CAPLAN et al.

No. 75108.

> **Mark the first cite with one asterisk, mark the second cite with two asterisks.** ☞

*
184 Ga. App. 567, 362 S.E.2d 103
**

Oct. 5, 1987.

**104 Joseph B. Bergen, Frederick S. Bergen, Savannah, for appellant.

William P. Franklin, Jr., Wendy W. Williamson, Savannah, for appellees.

*567 BANKE, Presiding Judge.

This is an appeal by the plaintiff from a grant of summary judgment to the defendants in an action to recover for alleged medical malpractice and intentional infliction of emotional distress.

The evidence, construed most favorably towards the plaintiff as respondent on motion for summary judgment, may be summarized as follows. Defendant Gerald E. Caplan, M.D., acting as a member and agent of defendant Radiology Associates, P.A., performed a series of radiological tests on the plaintiff for the purpose of investigating the cause of ab-dominal pains that she was experiencing. The tests were performed at the request of another physician who was responsible for the actual treatment of the plaintiff and who is not a party to this litigation. One of the possible diagnoses being investigated was cancer.

The procedures performed by Dr. Caplan revealed that a portion of the plaintiff's pancreas was abnormally enlarged, confirming the possibility of cancer but warranting no definite diagnosis in this regard. In his report to the plaintiff's treating physician, Dr. Caplan wrote: "Close follow-up evaluation of the uncinate of the head of the pancreas is recommended although hopefully the change seen is not a manifestation of a neoplasm." In preparing an insurance claim form for submission to the plaintiff's medical insurance carrier, however, Dr. Caplan inserted or caused to be inserted in the space designated, "Diagnosis of nature of illness or injury," the following language: "157.9 Pancreas: Determine Extent of Malignancy." Dr. Caplan chose this language in an effort to fit the plaintiff's insurance claim into one of the pre-ordained diagnostic categories considered compensable by her insurance carrier, and thereby to minimize the possibility that the claim would be rejected.

A copy of the insurance claim form subsequently came into the hands of the plaintiff, who, upon reading it, was led to believe that she had been diagnosed as having cancer.

She immediately telephoned Dr. Caplan's office to verify this and was assured by his staff that the language in question had been used solely to expedite payment of her insurance claim. She was additionally informed that only her treating physician was in a position to discuss her final diagnosis with her. The plaintiff did in fact discuss the results of her radiographic tests with her treating physician **105 and was assured by him that she did not have cancer; however, the fear and concern which she had experienced upon reading the insurance form nevertheless did not abate.

The plaintiff does not argue in this appeal that Dr. Caplan's conduct constituted medical malpractice; however, she does urge in

> **Note the page change for the S.E.2d reporter, above, identified by two asterisks, and the page change for the Georgia Appeals Reports, identified below by one asterisk.**

her *568 brief that he may be held liable in tort for intentional infliction of emotional distress based on the "negligent misinformation" which he caused to be transmitted to her.

☞ **It is a contradiction in terms to base a claim for intentional infliction of emotional distress on mere "negligent misinformation."** A cause of action for intentional infliction of emotional distress must be predicated on misconduct of an outrageous or egregious nature, which is "so terrifying or insulting as naturally to humiliate, embarrass or frighten the plaintiff." *Ga. Power Co. v. Johnson*, 155 Ga. App. 862, 863, 274 S.E.2d 17 (1980). [FN1] Clearly, Dr. Caplan's conduct in this case does not fall into this category. Indeed, it borders on the ridiculous to suggest that it was his intention to cause the plaintiff emotional distress or that he was engaged in some nefarious scheme to make money at the expense of her mental and emotional well being. Quite obviously, Dr. Caplan had no intention of terrorizing, harassing, or insulting the plaintiff but sought merely to avoid problems with her health insurance carrier, for her benefit as well as his own.

FN1. See, e.g., *American Fin. & Loan Corp. v. Coots*, 105 Ga.App. 849, 125 S.E.2d 689 (1962) (recovery authorized against bill collector who terrorized plaintiff and his family at gunpoint); *Delta Fin. Co. v. Ganakas*, 93 Ga.App. 297, 91 S.E.2d 383 (1956) (recovery allowed against defendant whose agent threatened small child with arrest in attempt to repossess her parents' television set); and *Stephens v. Waits*, 53 Ga.App.

44, 184 S.E. 781 (1936) (recovery allowed against defendants who physically intimidated plaintiffs as they were attempting to bury family member).

The cases relied upon by the plaintiff are quite distinguishable from the case before us and provide no support whatever for a recovery in this case. In *Greer v. Medders*, 176 Ga.App. 408, 336 S.E.2d 328 (1985), recovery was authorized against a physician who had verbally abused and insulted a patient and the patient's wife as the patient lay in a hospital bed attempting to recover from recent surgery. In *Chuy v. Philadelphia Eagles Football Club*, 595 F.2d 1265 (3rd Cir.1979), a case which is not, in any event, binding on this court, the defendant physician inexplicably made a false announcement to the press that the plaintiff, a professional football player, was suffering from a fatal disease, knowing such was not the case. Although in *Stafford v. Neurological Med., Inc.*, 811 F.2d 470 (8th Cir.1987), the defendant physician's alleged misconduct was virtually identical to that alleged in the present case, the patient there did not merely suffer emotional distress as a result of the physician's misstatement on the insurance form, she committed suicide. Consequently, the plaintiff there was not limited to a recovery for intentional infliction of emotional distress but was authorized to recover on the basis of mere negligence.

Judgment affirmed.

Index of *Bluebook* Rules

Whitepages Rules

Rule 1.1, 123
Rule 1.2, 126
Rule 1.3, 129
Rule 1.4, 123, 126, 129
Rule 1.5, 131
Rule 1.5(b), 66
Rule 3, 17, 101, 106
Rule 3.1(c), 24
Rule 3.2(a), 18, 35
Rule 3.2(b), 22
Rule 3.2(c), 23
Rule 3.3, 19, 21
Rule 4, 26, 77, 97, 109, 125
Rule 4.1, 26, 52, 78
Rule 4.1–4.2, 102
Rule 4.2, 27
Rule 5.1, 135
Rule 5.1(a), 136
Rule 5.1(b), 136
Rule 5.2, 137
Rule 5.3, 139
Rule 6.1, 24
Rule 6.2(a), 149
Rule 6.2(b), 151
Rule 6.2(c–d), 151
Rule 8, 143
Rule 10, 30
Rule 10.1.1(vi), 15
Rule 10.2.1, 30, 40
Rule 10.2.1(a), 40, 47
Rule 10.2.1(b), 47

Rule 10.2.1(c), 40
Rule 10.2.1(e), 47
Rule 10.2.1(f), 42
Rule 10.2.1(h), 40
Rule 10.2.1(i), 51
Rule 10.2.1(j), 52
Rule 10.2.2, 30, 40
Rule 10.3, 33
Rule 10.3.1, 58
Rule 10.3.1(a), 77
Rule 10.3.2, 35
Rule 10.3.3, 59
Rule 10.4, 36
Rule 10.5, 39
Rule 10.6, 62
Rule 10.6.1, 62, 64
Rule 10.6.3, 63
Rule 10.6.4, 66
Rule 10.7, 65
Rule 10.8, 155, 156
Rule 10.8.1, 157
Rule 10.9, 52, 53
Rule 11, 163
Rule 11, 81, 82
Rule 12, 68
Rule 12.1–12.3, 70
Rule 12.10, 77, 78, 79
Rule 12.10(d), 161
Rule 12.3, 70
Rule 12.3.1(c), 77
Rule 12.3.1(d), 74

Rule 12.3.2, 75
Rule 12.5, 160
Rule 12.9.1, 88, 90
Rule 12.9.3, 93, 94, 95, 165
Rule 12.9.4, 108, 168
Rule 14.2, 85
Rule 14.4, 164
Rule 15, 99
Rule 15.1, 100
Rule 15.2, 101
Rule 15.3, 101
Rule 15.4, 101, 102
Rule 15.8, 110, 114, 168
Rule 15.9, 166, 170

Rule 15.10, 102, 111, 114
Rule 16, 103
Rule 16.2, 104
Rule 16.3, 104
Rule 16.4, 105, 106
Rule 16.7.6, 112
Rule 16.8, 167, 169
Rule 16.9, 106, 113
Rule 18.2, 160, 164
Rule 18.2.1, 160, 161, 166
Rule 18.3, 155, 156, 160, 166, 167
Rule 18.3.1, 157
Rule 18.8, 161, 164

Bluepages Rules

Rule B1.1, 12, 123
Rule B1.2, 126
Rule B1.3, 131
Rule B2, 6
Rule B5.1, 135
Rule B8, 143, 145, 146, 147
Rule B10, 30
Rule B10.1.1, 30, 47
Rule B10.1.2, 33, 35
Rule B10.1.3, 36, 39, 58
Rule B10.1.4, 155, 156
Rule B10.1.5, 62, 64
Rule B10.1.6, 65
Rule B10.2, 53
Rule B11, 81, 82
Rule B12, 68

Rule B12.1, 70, 160
Rule B12.1.3, 93, 94, 108
Rule B12.1.4, 88, 90
Rule B12.2, 77, 78, 79
Rule B14, 85, 87
Rule B15, 99
Rule B15.1, 110
Rule B15.2, 102
Rule B16, 103
Rule B16.2, 106
Rule B17, 117
Rule B17.1.1, 118
Rule B17.1.2, 21, 119
Rule B17.2, 120
Rule BT2.2, 94
Rule BT2.2, 95

Subject Index

Academic Style, generally: 6–8

Administrative Regulations
See Regulations

American Law Reports (A.L.R.) Annotations
generally: 112–13
electronic source: 169–70
short forms: 113

Books
See Treatises and Books

Capitalization
generally: 143–45
court documents: 145–48
court proceedings: 147
courts: 145–46
document titles: 147
judges & justices: 147–48
parties: 146

Cases
generally: 29–30
case names: *see* Cases, Names
citing parentheticals: 63–64
concurrences, citing: 62
dissents, citing: 62
electronic sources: 155–60
embedded citations: 15–16, 41
explanatory parentheticals: 131–33
ordering multiple parentheticals: 66
parallel citations: 58–59
public domain citations: 59–61
quoting parentheticals: 63–64
short forms: *see* Cases, Short Forms
star paging: 156–57
subsequent history: 65

unpublished cases: 157–59
weight of authority: 64

Cases, Court Information
generally: 36–39
when to omit: 37–38

Cases, Electronic Sources
generally: 155
published cases: 156–57
star paging: 156–57
unpublished cases: 153–55

Cases, Names
generally: 30
abbreviations: 41
acronyms: 42
actions and parties: 31–32
alternate names (d/b/a etc.): 47
businesses and organizations: 40–41
capacity, *see* descriptive terms
city, town or county as a party: 46
Commissioner, International Revenue
Service: 52
descriptive terms & phrases: 47–48, 50
double business designation rule: 40–41
embedded citations: 42
et al.: 32
geographical terms: 42–46
government as a party: 42–46
hyphenated surnames: 31
individuals: 31
Internal Revenue Service (IRS): 52
introductory phrases: 50–51
multiple actions: 32
multiple parties: 31
procedural phrases: 47–50

state or commonwealth as a party: 44–45
"the" in case names: 41
unions as a party: 51
United States government as a party: 43

Cases, Short Forms
generally: 52
alternate: 53–55
frequent (common) litigants: 54
id.: 26–27, 52–53
parallel citations: 58–59
unpublished cases: 159

Cases, Source Information
generally: 33
beginning page number: 35
first page, citing: 18, 35
multiple pages, citing: 18, 35
parallel citations: 58–59
pinpoint page number: 17–19, 35
reporter, correct reporter to cite: 33–34
reporter name: 35
star paging: 156–57
unpublished cases: 158–59
volume: 35

Cases, Year of Decision: 39

Citation Clauses, generally: 14–15

Citation Placement
see also specific authorities
generally: 10–16
citation clauses, generally: 14–15
citation sentences, generally: 14
embedded citations, generally: 15–16
split citations, generally: 16
when to cite: 10–11

Citation Sentences, generally: 14

"Citing" Parentheticals: 63–64

Comma, use of in numerals: 149–50

Common (Frequent) Litigants: 54

Concurrences, citing: 62

Constitutions:
generally: 81
electronic sources: 163–64
short forms: 82–83

Court Rules
See Procedural and Court Rules

Dictionaries
generally: 110
electronic source: 168–69
short forms: 111

Dissents, citing: 62

Electronic Sources
generally: 153
A.L.R. Annotations: 169–70
alternate practitioners' form, defined: 154
cases: 155–60
constitutions: 163–64
currency date, statutes: 161
dictionaries: 168–69
encyclopedias: 170
periodicals: 167–68
procedural and court rules: 165–66
regulations: 164–65
restatements: 168
star paging: 156–57
statutes: 160–63
treatises and books: 166–67
unpublished decisions: 157–59

Embedded Citations, generally: 15–16

Emphasis Added: 137

Encyclopedias
generally: 114–15
electronic source: 170
short forms: 114

En Dashes: 17

Endnotes, citing: 23–24

Et al.: 32

Explanatory Parentheticals: 131–32

Federal Appendix: 160

Footnotes, citing: 22–23

Frequent (common) Litigants: 54

Hyphens: 17

Id.
  generally: 26–27
  See also specific authorities

Internal Revenue Code: 88–89

Italics, typeface convention: 6–8

Large and Small Capitals, use of: 6–7

Law Reviews and Journals
  See Periodicals

Litigation Documents and Record Citations
  generally: 117
  multiple documents with same title: 118–19
  parentheses, enclosing in: 121–22
  pinpoints: 119–20
  short forms: 120–21
  title, document: 118–19

Local Rules of Court
  See also Procedural and Court Rules
  generally: 9
  how to find: 9

Medium Neutral Citations
  See Public Domain Citations

Multiple Case Parentheticals, ordering: 66

Non–Published Cases
  See Unpublished Cases

Numbers and Numerals
  generally: 149
  ordinals: 151

Ordinals: 151

Pages, citing multiple: 18

Paragraphs, multiple: 21

Parallel Citations: 58–59

Parentheticals
  See Cases or Explanatory Parentheticals

Periodicals
  generally: 103–04
  author(s): 104
  electronic source: 167–68
  periodical name: 105–06
  pinpoints: 106
  short forms: 106–07
  title: 104–05
  volume: 105
  year: 106

Pinpoints (Pincites)
  See also specific source
  generally: 17
  endnotes: 23–24
  footnotes: 22–23
  hyphens and dashes, using: 17
  lines: 21–22
  pages: 18–19
  paragraphs: 21
  sections: 19–21
  supplements: 24

Practitioners' Style, generally: 6–8

Procedural & Court Rules
  generally: 93
  electronic sources: 161–62
  finding court rules: 9
  rules of court, federal: 95–96
  rules of court, state: 96–97
  rules of evidence, federal: 93–94
  rules of evidence, state: 94–95
  rules of procedure federal: 93–94
  rules of procedure, state: 94–95
  short forms: 97–98

Public Domain Citations: 59–61

Quotations
  generally: 135
  alterations: 137–38
  block quotations: 136
  ellipses: 139
  omissions: 139–41
  short quotations: 136–37

Quoting Parentheticals: 63–64

Record Citations
  See Litigation Documents and Record
    Citations

Regulations
  generally: 85
  administrative, federal: 85–86
  administrative, state: 87–88
  electronic sources: 164–65
  Internal Revenue Code: 88–89
  short forms: *see* specific type of
    regulation
  Treasury: 90–91

Reporters
  See Cases, Source Information

Restatements
  generally: 108
  electronic source: 168
  short forms: 109

Rules of Procedure
  See Procedural and Court Rules

Secondary Sources
  See specific authority

Sections, citing multiple: 19–20

Sentences, citation, generally: 14

Short Forms
  See also specific authorities
  generally: 26
  alternate short forms, generally: 28

id., generally: 26–27
supra, generally: 28

Signals
  generally: 126–27
  combining signals: 127
  description of individual signals: 127–28
  explanatory parentheticals: 131–32
  multiple signals in strings: 129–30
  short forms with signals: 131
  signal types and ranks: 129–30

Single Adjacent Capitals
  see Spacing in Citations

Small Capitals, use of: 7–8

Spacing in Citations: 24–25

Split Citations: 16, 55

Star Paging: 156–57

Statutes
  generally: 67
  alternate short form: 79–80
  code name: 70–71
  code year: 75–76
  electronic sources: 160–63
  id.: 78
  multiple sections or subsections: 20–21,
    73–74
  named statutes: 77
  publisher: 74–75
  sections: 71–74
  short forms: 77–80
  subject matter codes: 77
  subsections: 20–21, 73–74
  supplements: 24, 76
  titles or chapters: 71–72
  year: 75–76

String Citations:
  generally: 123
  order of multiple authorities: 124–25
  short forms in string citations: 125–26

Subsequent History: 65

Supplements, generally: 24

Supra
    see also specific authorities
    generally: 27

Symbols
    generally: 151–52
    creating: 152
    dollar signs: 151
    paragraph: 151
    percent: 151
    section: 151

Treasury Regulations: 90–91

Treatises and Books
    generally: 99
    author(s): 100

electronic source: 166–67
    pinpoints: 101
    publication information: 101–02
    short forms: 102–03
    title: 101
    year: 102

Typeface Conventions
    generally: 6–8
    italics: 6–8
    large and small capitals: 7
    underlining: 6–8

Underlining, typeface convention: 6–8

Unpublished Cases
    see Electronic Sources

Weight of Authority: 64

CPSIA information can be obtained
at www.ICGtesting.com
Printed in the USA
LVHW010014070921
697099LV00003B/11